THE
VILLA-LOBOS
LETTERS

THE
VILLA-LOBOS
LETTERS

Edited, Translated
and Annotated by
LISA M. PEPPERCORN

Musicians in Letters
No. 1

TOCCATA
PRESS

First published in 1994 by Toccata Press.
This edition © Lisa M. Peppercorn, 1994.

British Library Cataloguing in Publication Data
Villa-Lobos, Heitor, *1887–1959*
  The Villa-Lobos letters. - (Musicians in letters)
  I. Title II. Peppercorn, Lisa M. II. Series
  780.92.

ISBN 0 907689 28 0
ISBN 0 907689 29 9 (pbk)
ISSN 0960 0094

Typeset in Plantin by York House Typographic Ltd, London
Printed and bound by SRP Ltd., Exeter

Contents

List of Illustrations

List of Facsimiles

Introduction

The letters of Heitor Villa-Lobos and his correspondents collected in this book cover a period of a little more than thirty
years. The earliest letter dates from 2 March 1927 and the
last from 2 September 1958.

The first extant letter of Villa-Lobos was written in Paris,
where the composer and his wife Lucília had settled for a
three-and-a-half year sojourn, sponsored by two Brazilian
industrialists and philanthropists, Arnaldo (1884–1964) and
Carlos (1883–1969) Guinle. Eighteen months before Villa-
Lobos' death the correspondence draws to a close, in an
exchange with the Pan American Union in the United States,
the country that was largely responsible for his rise to international fame after World War II. And it ends where it
began, in Paris, with three letters to Pierre Vidal.

The Villa-Lobos Letters brings together all those pieces of
correspondence I have been able to locate, despite attempts
to locate others that must exist. Enquiries to artists once
linked with the composer (and most must now be advanced
in years), as those to universities, libraries, radio stations, orchestral managements, concert agents, and the like all met
with the same reply – where any was forthcoming: no letters
to be found anywhere. Nothing rules out the possibility, of
course, that other letters may be discovered, somewhere, at
some time. And it will be seen that this collection contains
virtually only letters from Villa-Lobos, which suggests that
his addressees kept his letters, while he threw theirs out.

In a surprising contrast with the exuberance of his music,
and with the personality revealed in many of the photographs
of Villa-Lobos, his letters are often short, almost bare –
indeed, their very paucity compares strikingly with his vol-
uminous output of music. The explanation may well be

found in an aside in a letter to his wife (LETTER 19, p. 49): 'you know very well that I hate writing letters'.

The letters he did write reveal a talent for making friends with a mixture of charm and diplomatic calculation, and a complete absence of the grand manner. They also underline the extent to which his life was geared to the composition and performance of his works, for they deal almost exclusively with his music. They are professional rather than personal communications, even when written to long-standing friends, such as Irving Schwerké, Serge Koussevitzky or Florent Schmitt – indeed, Villa-Lobos' restraint in burdening others with his own personal problems may account for part of the charm that endeared him to so many people. Except for two references to his serious cancer operations, and those only in passing, the letters never betray his sentiments; they neither refer to his private life, offer personal observations, nor comment on friends or family. They are dispassionate, unemotional, even cool. Villa-Lobos restricts himself strictly to professional matters, past or prospective performances of his music, to questions of money or of concert plans. His letters – even most of those exchanged with his wife – may thus be categorised almost as business correspondence. The exceptions are the three written by the composer and Lucília at the time of their estrangement which touch on the personal difficulties of their separation. Yet here, too, Villa-Lobos was at pains not to reveal – to any outsider, at least – the real reasons behind his decision.

My principal aim in translating and annotating these letters is to offer source material, in the hope that it may form a useful contribution to Villa-Lobos scholarship. The sources reproduced in this book include: facsimile letters; facsimile manuscript first pages of some of the compositions discussed in the letters; facsimiles of some of the programmes cited in the correspondence, authenticating details of dates and places of performances sometimes misreported in other reference books; photographs of Villa-Lobos' addressees and others mentioned in the letters; and an 'iconography' of objects and places to which they refer.

Villa-Lobos in 1956, three years before his death, at his home in Rio de Janeiro (courtesy of the Museu Villa-Lobos)

Here the correspondence is organised chronologically, except where commonsense has occasionally required that several letters addressed to the same person or topic be published together.

Circumstances conspired to ensure that Villa-Lobos' correspondence with Arnaldo and Carlos Guinle could form only a sketchy part of this book. In 1939 I was fortunate enough, when I was living in Rio de Janeiro (from the late 1930s to early '60s) to have been able, with the Guinles' permission, to copy these letters by hand.

There were thirteen communications altogether, dating from 2 March 1927 to 7 February 1931. Quotations from this exchange can be found in my biography of Villa-Lobos[1] but, alas, when moving back from Brazil to Europe, my archives and books were lost in transit and with them my handwritten copies of the Guinle-Villa-Lobos correspondence. I therefore tried to recover it, but failed. The executors of the Guinle estate knew nothing about the matter. The Guinle heirs claimed to have given the letters to the Brazilian Ministry of Education and Culture – which professed no knowledge of any such donation. With the help of some friends I managed to contact by letter (25 August 1980) the son of Carlos Guinle's secretary; he replied (9 September) that he remembered that his father, shortly before his death, had shown him the Villa-Lobos letters, together with letters by others that he judged to be of importance for posterity, with the request that his son take good care of them after his death. The son promised to search for the letters among his father's papers and holdings and, since he was most interested in this matter himself and a true admirer of Villa-Lobos, he continued, he would contact me immediately if he found them. This was the first and last I heard from him, despite several reminders on my part.

A single letter from the correspondence is still available. It was in the estate of Villa-Lobos' wife, Lucília, and is

---

[1] *Heitor Villa-Lobos: Leben und Werk des brasilianischen Komponisten*, Atlantis, Zurich, 1972, pp. 71–95.

addressed to Arnaldo Guinle; it is incorporated in this volume (LETTER 12, pp. 31–34). The bulk, therefore, of the Guinle-Villa-Lobos correspondence must be considered lost except for those parts translated in my biography; these are reproduced here (marked with an asterisk for the sake of clarity), now translated into English from my German translation of the Portuguese originals.

Virtually all the letters in this book speak for themselves. I have therefore confined my comments to occasional explanation of facts or of the circumstances that led to the writing of the letters, or to give details of people cited in them. The translations, where possible without exaggeration, attempt to mirror the idiosyncracies of Villa-Lobos' originals, which are mainly in Portuguese and French; where he dated in Portuguese a letter in French or English this has been retained. His own English is reproduced unaltered.

Acknowledgements

I am much indebted to the many individuals and institutions who have lent their valuable assistance in obtaining these letters and photographs, and herewith express my gratitude to them all for their generous help. They are too numerous to be detailed here, although many are identified in the footnotes. For permission to reproduce the letters in this book I am indebted to the following:

United States Music Division, The Library of Congress, Washington DC, with the consent of the late Arminda Villa-Lobos, Rio de Janeiro, Brazil, for the correspondence with Serge Koussevitzky (LETTERS 30, 32–34, and the telegrams on p. 82) and with Harold Spivacke (telegrams on p. 78, LETTER 31) and the letters to Irving Schwerké (5, 9, 10, 13 and 48–55) and Nicolas Slonimsky (28, 29); Dance Collection, Astor, Lenox and Tilden Foundations, The New York Public Library, with the consent of Janet Collins, Seattle, for the letters to Janet Collins (72–75), and its Music Division, with the consent of Arminda Villa-Lobos, for the letters to Frederick Jacobi (27) and to Claire Raphael Reis (77); the Organization of American States, Washington DC, for the correspondence with Guillermo Espinosa (78–80); the Boston Symphony Orchestra, for the letter on behalf of the Serge Koussevitzky Music Foundation in the Library of Congress, Washington DC (76); the Louisville Orchestra Records, University of Louisville Archives and Records Center, Louisville, Kentucky, for the correspondence with the Louisville Orchestra (60–71); Janet Collins, Seattle, for extracts from a letter to the editor; Aldo Parisot, New Haven, Connecticut, for letters from Villa-Lobos (58–59) and a letter from Mr Parisot to the editor; Bernardo Segáll, Sherman Oaks, California, for extracts from a letter to the editor; the editor of *The Journal of Musicological Research*, for permission to reproduce the translation of the letter to Laurinda Santos Lobo (26), which first appeared in its pages, and the editor of *The Latin American Music Review*, in whose pages the letter (57) to Florent Schmitt and his wife was first published (in facsimile).

Canada   Ellen Ballon Papers, University Archives, Dalhousie University Library, Halifax, Nova Scotia, for the letters to Ellen Ballon (35, 37–40 and the telegram on p. 105); Ralph Gustafson, North Hatley, Quebec, for letters from Villa-Lobos (36, 41–43) and for two letters to the editor (Appendix Two, pp. 195–99).

Brazil   Oldemar Guimarães, Rio de Janeiro, for a letter to Arnaldo Guinle (12) and for Villa-Lobos' correspondence with his wife Lucília (17–25).

United Kingdom   BBC Written Archives Centre, Caversham Park, Reading, with the consent of Arminda Villa-Lobos, for the letters to Edward Lockspeiser (45) and Peter Crossley-Holland (47), the letter from Peter Crossley-Holland to Villa-Lobos (46), the extract of a letter from the British Council (44), and two programmes from the BBC Third Programme (5 and 17 March 1949); and the editor of *Music and Letters* for permission to reproduce my translations of some of the letters from Villa-Lobos to his wife (17–23) and the two letters from Lucília to her husband (24 and 25, pp. 57–63).

France   Music Department, Bibliothèque Nationale, Paris, with the consent of Arminda Villa-Lobos, for the letters to Florent Schmitt (57) and Laurinda Santos Lobo (26); UNESCO, Paris, for the letter to Luiz Heitor Corrêa de Azevedo (56); Pierre Vidal, Paris, for the three letters to him from Villa-Lobos (81–83).

Italy   The editor of *Studi Musicali* for permission to reproduce the translation of the letter (12) to Arnaldo Guinle.

For help with the proof-reading I am grateful to Sharon Jackson and Guy Rickards.

PART I

THE PULL
OF PARIS

In 1923–24 Villa-Lobos had spent a year in Paris on a Brazilian government grant, and at the beginning of 1927 he settled there again, at 11 place St Michel. From Paris he wrote three letters to the Guinle brothers, one on 2 March to Arnaldo, another, undated, to Carlos, and a third, on 20 April, again to Carlos. They dealt with publishing matters: one concerned folk and children's songs, collected in Brazil by a group financed by the Guinles who intended, after Villa-Lobos had finished editing the material at the brothers' request, to publish it at their own expense. This publication, which Villa-Lobos had intended to call *Alma Brasileira* (*Brazilian Soul*), failed to materialise. The collection was never returned to the Guinles, as Carlos once explained to me sadly, and it mysteriously disappeared. In the same letter Villa-Lobos asked for an additional fund of 20,000 francs, even though his travelling expenses and monthly allowance allowed him and Lucília a comfortable life in Paris.

LETTER 1*
VILLA-LOBOS TO ARNALDO GUINLE
Original: Portuguese

[Paris, 2 March 1927]

The second volume devoted to nursery rhymes and the most varied songs from the hinterland is almost ready, and I hope to finish it this year [...]. In a few days I shall go to Vienna to participate in the musical congress [...]. This lecture [one he intended to give there] is a short and simple summary of my entire plan for our work *Alma Brasileira*. [...] I am totally confused and fear a financial disaster [...].

The second and third letters, to Carlos Guinle, concerned Villa-Lobos' efforts to have his music published by Éditions Max Eschig in Paris.[1] He announced that Eschig had offered him a contract, with a view to publishing the Second and Third Piano Trios, Third

---

[1] *Cf.* Peppercorn, *op. cit.*, pp. 71–95.

String Quartet, Second Cello Sonata, *Chôros* Nos. 2, 7 and 10, the Trio for oboe, clarinet and bassoon, and 'Teiru' and 'Canide Ioune-Sabath' from the *Três Poemas Indígenas*, and *Na Bahia Tem* for *a cappella* chorus. But Villa-Lobos was supposed to contribute something towards the costs of publication – which, of course, he did not have.[2] Eschig, he continued, were convinced of the success of his works.

LETTER 2*
VILLA-LOBOS TO CARLOS GUINLE
Original: Portuguese

[Paris, undated]

I received a proposition from the publishers to print ten further works but without paying advance royalties [...].

Upon receipt of Guinle's reply and the subsidy necessary to finance the venture, the composer wrote again to Carlos, telling him that the amount earmarked for it had already been withdrawn from the account that had been opened for him.

LETTER 3*
VILLA-LOBOS TO CARLOS GUINLE
Original: Portuguese

[Paris, 20 April 1927]

[It was decided] to publish nineteen of my works [...], fifteen of these within the short period of one year, the rest six months after the completion of the production devoted to the first fifteen [...].

[2] The contract with Éditions Max Eschig, signed early in April 1927, included, in addition to the works mentioned above, the First Cello Concerto (*cf.* p. 134) and the *Nonetto*. Max Eschig (1872–1927), then still running the company that bears his name, requested 'that Villa-Lobos or another person subsidise by 50% the first publication of these thirteen works' (letter to me from Gérald Hugon, Éditions Max Eschig, dated 12 May 1989). Villa-Lobos' first contract with Eschig had been signed on 8 October 1924; it involved the *Suite* for voice and violin, which appeared in print the next year.

*Carlos Guinle
(courtesy of* O
Cruzeiro, *Rio de
Janeiro)*

[It was suggested] to give two important concerts in which
the larger part of these works should be performed [...]
supported by the firm[3] and some of my friends and
patrons. [...]

I must now explain to you my reasons for having to super-
vise and observe the work on this publication. As my tech-
nique and method of composition is entirely different from
the usual one, and as it is my intention to help the printers
and engravers with quickly needed advice when they don't
know what to do, it is inevitable that I should stay at least
until the two contracts have been completed. This will take

[3] That is, Éditions Max Eschig.

twenty months from the day the first of the works appears in
print. [...]

   Although the Guinles had intended to subsidise Villa-Lobos'
stay for only a few months or a season, Carlos gave way and, accepting
Villa-Lobos' reasons, enabled him to remain in Paris.
   The two concerts mentioned in LETTER 3 were indeed given in
Paris, on 24 October and 5 December, and were announced as
'Deux Festivals consacrés aux œuvres de Villa-Lobos'.
   On 9 December 1927 Villa-Lobos again wrote[4] to Carlos Guinle
about his plans for extended trips to other European countries,
although they did not bear fruit at the time. Since he was not certain that Carlos would give him the financial help he required, he
had also turned to other patrons in Rio de Janeiro and São Paulo
who had previously helped him organise concerts in Brazil. Disap-
pointed with the response, he wrote again to Guinle.

LETTER 4*
VILLA-LOBOS TO CARLOS GUINLE
Original: Portuguese

[Paris, 9 December 1927]

Only D. Laurinda Santos Lobo[5] and our Arnaldo [Guinle]
answered properly and immediately. [...] the others remained absolutely silent. I don't know why [...].

   On 2 February 1928 he wrote to Carlos Guinle[6] that he would
have to remain in Paris for at least another two years and asked for

---

[4] Not quoted in Peppercorn, *op. cit.*

[5] Laurinda Santos Lobo was a Brazilian socialite and patroness of the arts.
She was described by Luiz Heitor Corrêa de Azevedo, the eminent Brazilian musicologist (*cf.* pp. 126–27 and 155), thus (in a letter to me, dated 3
August 1982):
   I knew Dona Laurinda Santos Lobo well [...]. I was often in her
   home in Santa Tereza [a part of Rio de Janeiro]. She was a lady of
   forceful temperament who liked to receive artists in her home as
   though they were flowers to adorn it. The fact is what she really
   believed in was the undisputed superiority of money above all other
   things. She dragged behind her a husband with no voice in this
   chapter, docile like a little domestic dog.
Cf. also LETTER 26, p. 65.

[6] Not quoted in Peppercorn, *op. cit.*

further financial support; Guinle agreed and provided the necessary grants for another year.

Towards the end of 1927 Villa-Lobos had entered into communication with Irving Schwerké (1893–1975), the American writer, pianist and teacher who, from 1920, had lived first in Madrid and then in Paris as music correspondent for a number of foreign publications; he returned to the United States in 1941. In 1927 Schwerké had published in Paris a book entitled *Kings, Jazz and David.*[7] This collection of essays included one on the Brazilian composer, originally published in *The League of Composers Review*, in New York, January 1925;[8] it is entitled 'Villa-Lobos: Rabelais of Modern Music' and is dedicated to Vera Janacópulos (1892–1955), the Brazilian singer who lived in Paris for many years and who, in 1921, had performed some of Villa-Lobos' songs there. Schwerké had sent Villa-Lobos the book as a gift. The response was oddly calm: most composers would be more obviously grateful for such lengthy attention, especially when he was still little known in Paris – and only one major concert of his music had taken place that year, the first of the 'Deux Festivals', on 24 October, to be followed by the other on 5 December.

LETTER 5
VILLA-LOBOS TO IRVING SCHWERKÉ
Original: French

Paris 27/11/927

Dear Mr Irving Schwerke
I have received your book and thank you for the article which you have dedicated to me. I promise to read your publication with much interest and give you later my impression of your work. I shall be very happy to see you at the next

---

[7] Privately printed for the author by Les Presses modernes, Paris.

[8] The League of Composers was founded in 1923 in New York City by members of the International Composers' Guild to promote compositions and performances of contemporary music; it merged with the International Society for Contemporary Music (ISCM) in 1954. It commissioned 110 works and published a quarterly review, *Modern Music*, from 1924 until 1946 (*cf. The New Grove Dictionary of American Music*, Macmillan, London and New York, 1986, Vol. III, p. 22).

concert dedicated to my works, on 5 December, at the Salle
Gaveau.

Cordially

11 Place St. Michel   Villa-Lobos

This letter, the first of twelve to Schwerké, began a friendship
which can be documented until 1953, when it was discontinued –
not, apparently, by design but more probably because of Villa-
Lobos' heavy travelling schedule after the Second World War, to
conduct in the United States and Europe. In Paris the correspondence was resumed only in April 1929.

In the previous year, 1928, Villa-Lobos and the Guinle brothers
had again exchanged letters on more urgent matters. He acknow-
ledged their further subsidy to prolong his stay in Paris, expressing
worry about his health in the same letter (Villa-Lobos to Carlos
Guinle, 2 February), a theme to which he returned a month later:
'The state of my health has also caused some expenses' (Villa-Lobos
to Carlos Guinle, 12 March). That same day he wrote to Arnaldo,
mentioning his health again, but also informing him of North
American interest in his music. No performance resulted from the
letter he mentions, although, a few months later, on 23 and 24
November 1928, Leopold Stokowski did conduct the Philadelphia
Orchestra in Villa-Lobos' *Danças Características Africanas*, probably
the first North American performance of any of his orchestral
works.

LETTER 6*
VILLA-LOBOS TO ARNALDO GUINLE
Original: Portuguese

[Paris, 12 March 1928]

The state of my health is gradually improving [...].

I received a letter from New York in which I am told that
the Pan American Association of Composers will give a concert devoted exclusively to my works for small orchestra, that
is to say, all my *Chôros* compositions which have appeared in
print, and some vocal and orchestral music. [...] This means
that I shall shortly be in North America at their expense.

Irving Schwerké
(courtesy of the
Music Division,
Library of Congress)

The letter continues with the information that the Director of the Paris Opéra was interested in some of the stage works of Villa-Lobos, who felt that

In my opinion the genre of opera is a grave for a composer who has a broad vision, and I prefer to become famous one day with my *Chôros* compositions instead of as a writer of popular operas. Seen from the artistic point of view the latter has no solid foundation.

Wagner was acclaimed only after thirty years, continued Villa-Lobos, who hoped

to make a fortune with my 'music of the suburb' in these thirty years [...].

In the spring of the following year Villa-Lobos sent an almost euphoric letter to Arnaldo Guinle – but all the projected performances he mentions failed to materialise.

LETTER 7*
VILLA-LOBOS TO ARNALDO GUINLE
Original: Portuguese

[Paris, 14 April 1929]

Today I can confirm to you that in Berlin, Munich and Leipzig [...] some of my works will be performed in October. The publisher Eschig has already received an order for orchestral material, for the chorus, etc. [...] In March or April I myself will go to Berlin to conduct my new works at the expenses of B. Schott' & Sons [...]!

[...] I believe what I still miss is a visit to London and to go from there with some assurance to North America. This will probably be the last stage of my way to a material independence from your protection.

In the same letter Villa-Lobos added that he intended to come to Brazil for a short visit in 1929, together with Lucília, and wanted to give concerts in São Paulo and Rio de Janeiro, as well as in several states in the north of Brazil. He hoped that by becoming the official guest of the governors of these states he would obtain free passage for himself and those in his group on the vessels of the Brazilian shipping company, Lóide Brasileira. He also wrote that

To secure my success I am bringing with me an outstanding Belgian violinist[9]

and he requested Guinle further to underwrite this artist's travelling expenses and stay in Brazil. He also asked Guinle for additional funds to buy himself a cello, and wanted Arnaldo to take the necessary steps to publicise his homecoming. And, as if these demands were not enough, he asked Guinle to guarantee the funds

[9] Maurice Raskin (born 1906).

for a series of concerts in São Paulo and Rio de Janeiro, because he believed that

These would be the key to our journey to the North.

And Guinle, indeed, came up with the money. Yet in another letter of the same date, he writes of changes to his travel plans.

LETTER 8*
VILLA-LOBOS TO ARNALDO GUINLE
Original: Portuguese

[Paris, 14 April 1929]

[...] In short, I will not be able to go to Manaus as I had planned because I have been officially invited by the festival committee of the exhibition[10] to be in Barcelona this coming October.

He arrived in Barcelona on 14 October 1929 and conducted a concert there on 18 October.

A few days after writing to Arnaldo Guinle, Villa-Lobos sent two little notes to Irving Schwerké, dispatching them through the Paris pneumatic mail.[11] Both letters were sent to Schwerké's home at 18 rue Juliette Lamber, Paris 17ème.

---

[10] The Ibero-American Music Festival; another Brazilian composer, Oscar Lorenzo Fernândez (1897–1948), was also asked to participate.

The fourth concert of this festival, on 18 October 1929 in the Palacio Nacional, was exclusively devoted to works of Brazilian composers. The second part of this concert was directed by Villa-Lobos and included his *Amazonas*, *Chôros* No. 10 and *Três Poemas Indígenas* (Peppercorn, *op. cit.*, p. 90).

[11] The pneumatic postal service in Paris was installed during the Second Empire, under Napoleon III. It used underground tubes between post offices and was intended to offer a special-delivery mail service; inevitably, it became obsolete, and ceased operation on 1 April 1984.

LETTER 9
VILLA-LOBOS TO IRVING SCHWERKÉ
Original: French

Paris, 17/4/929

Dear friend
During the day of 18 next (Thursday) I shall be free only
from noon until 2.30 in the afternoon. Hence, I could accept
with pleasure your luncheon if [this] is convenient.
Well, till tomorrow without fail.

Cordially yours

Villa-Lobos

LETTER 10
VILLA-LOBOS TO IRVING SCHWERKÉ
Original: French

Friday 22 [1929]

Dear friend
Sundays are the days which I reserve to receive my friends
and to rest, from 2 until 5 o'clock in the afternoon.
If you like, give me this pleasure to see you Sunday next, or
we can fix an appointment.
11 Place St. Michel

Cordially yours

Villa-Lobos

After Villa-Lobos had accepted Schwerké's lunch invitation, the
composer in turn requested Schwerké's presence at his *jour fixe* the
following Sunday afternoon from 2 to 5 p.m. (It was Carlos Guinle,
so Villa-Lobos recounted,[12] who had suggested to him that he have
a *jour fixe* in Paris, then the custom there for making contact with
others.

[12] According to Arthur Rubinstein, in *My Many Years*, Jonathan Cape,
London, 1980, pp. 172–73.

A painting by Joaquim Roca, made in Paris in the 1920s,
of Villa-Lobos playing the cello (courtesy of the Museu Villa-Lobos)

The last letter surviving from 1929, if in fragmentary form, plays up rather to Arnaldo Guinle's generosity.

LETTER 11*
VILLA-LOBOS TO ARNALDO GUINLE
Original: Portuguese

[São Paulo, 12 September 1929]

My only real and genuine friend [...], in spite of the fact that I owe almost the whole of my good situation in Europe to the marks of favour and the protection of Dr Carlos, it is you who gave me abundant help even in that respect [...].

In early 1930 Villa-Lobos was beset by unexpected misfortune. He had recently made arrangements with the piano manufacturers Gaveau to promote the sale of their instruments.[13] But some misunderstanding must have occurred between the composer and Gaveau, because he could hardly wait for an important concert to take place before writing to Arnaldo Guinle to ask for his help. The letter was written the day after the premiere (on 23 February 1930) of Villa-Lobos' *Mômoprecóce* at the Salle Pleyel; the Orchestre Symphonique de Paris was conducted by Enrique Fernández Arbós,[14] with the Brazilian pianist Magda Tagliaferro as soloist.[15] LETTER 12, apparently the only one surviving from the exchange between Villa-Lobos and the Guinle brothers, was left in the estate of the composer's wife, Lucília Guimarães Villa-Lobos (1886–1966), and is currently in the possession of her brothers and sister,

[13] One of them, a model 3, No. 86.794, was bought, on 31 August 1936, by Arminda Villa-Lobos (1912–1985), the composer's companion during the last 23 years of his life, after he had separated from his estranged wife Lucília in 1936 (*cf.* pp. 56–63). This piano became the joint property of Arminda and the composer. After his death she donated the piano to the Museu Villa-Lobos in Rio de Janeiro.

[14] Arbós (1863–1939) began his career as a violinist, having studied with Vieuxtemps and Joachim, *inter alios*. He is perhaps best remembered nowadays for his brilliant orchestration of *Iberia* by Albéniz.

[15] Tagliaferro (1893–1986) was still giving concerts in the 1980s, when she was into her nineties.

Oldemar Guimarães, Luiz Guimarães, Alvaro de Oliveira Guimarães and Dinorah Guimarães Campos, in Rio de Janeiro.[16]

LETTER 12
VILLA-LOBOS TO ARNALDO GUINLE
Original: Portuguese

Paris 24/2/930

Dear Arnaldo
I waited until the 23rd inst. to write to you not only about the Gaveau pianos, but also to send you the latest news and the first reviews concerning the performance of my Fantasia for piano and orchestra – premiered yesterday by the Symphony Orchestra of Paris conducted by Arbós; it was very well received by the audience – as well as other previous reviews.
A few days ago I received a sort of call from the administration of the Maison Gaveau, though in very delicate terms, to settle my commitment in the amount of 80 . . . for the four pianos which I took to Brazil. They tell me that the administration of the M[aison] G[aveau] is going to close their books for this year; they absolutely counted on the good result of the sales in Brazil of the four pianos, which they entrusted to me, completely relying on my word. They expect me to go personally to one of their Directors or assume this obligation in writing.
It stunned me, as you may well imagine.
They waited precisely for the moment when the dates of my festivals are approaching to hold a knife to my throat.

---

[16] A facsimile of this letter, in its original Portuguese, was first published in a volume of reprints of concert programmes, reviews and photographs, which Villa-Lobos' in-laws had printed privately, at their own expense: *Villa-Lobos, Vista da Platéia e na Intimidade, 1912–1935*, Rio de Janeiro, 1972, pp. 337–39. The Portuguese original and my English translation, accompanied by my comments, were published in *Studi Musicali*, Vol. X, No. 1, Rome, 1981, pp. 171–79.

Manuscript first page of Mômoprecóce
(courtesy of Éditions Max Eschig)

As you may remember, the Maison Gaveau is offering me the large hall free and publicising my concerts as well; without this important support and prestige I couldn't realise any concert at present, since I have no material protection at this moment.

Now, it is absolutely impossible to give up these concerts in Paris at this time, because they mean the continuation of my artistic image in all of Europe. Otherwise, I shall be forgotten and all the excellent moral and artistic situation in which I find myself today will go down the drain.

I figure that the only solution of this case is the following: to find some one in Rio or São Paulo who is willing to lend me, against pledge of the pianos which have not yet been sold, the amount of 80 . . . and to deliver it to the Maison Gaveau as soon as possible, to avoid prejudicing the organisation of my festival next month.

The concert programme of 14 March 1930

According to the calculation which I left with Mário,[17] the four Gaveau pianos represent the following, in Brazilian currency, in my favour:

1	Grand Piano for Dr Carlos	14,867
2	Baby grand pianos	28,000
1	Grand Piano, the last three to be sent to D. Olivia Penteado[18]	12,000
		54,867

Deducting 16,000 francs which Dr Carlos advanced me in Paris 5,396

Deducting 4 Contos[19] which you paid on my behalf for the hotel expenses of Terán[20] and Raskin[21]..4,000

Deducting 2 Contos which D. Olivia was to give to Raskin for his return to Europe.................2,000

Deducting (what amounts to approximately 1,000 for expenses you may have for the pianos) 1,000

                                                            12,396

There remain 42,471 in my favour, which, converted into French francs, represent approximately 128,000 francs.

I then have a substantial amount at your disposal to let you find somebody there who at least lends me the sum that the Maison Gaveau asks from me for 30 March, which is simply 80 . . .

[17] Mário Polo was Arnaldo Guinle's secretary.

[18] Dona Olivia Guedes Penteado (1872–1934) was a São Paulo patroness of the arts.

[19] One conto is worth a thousand cruzeiros. At the time of Villa-Lobos' letter to Arnaldo Guinle the unit of currency in Brazil was the *milreis;* the name was changed to *cruzeiro* in 1942, to *cruzado* in February 1986, to *cruzado novo* in 1989, back to *cruzeiro* in March 1990 and to *cruzeiro real* on 2 August 1993.

[20] Tomás Terán (1896–1964), a Brazilian pianist of Spanish origin, lived in Brazil from 1929. He had a considerable influence on many younger Brazilian pianists.

[21] *Cf.* note 9 on p. 26.

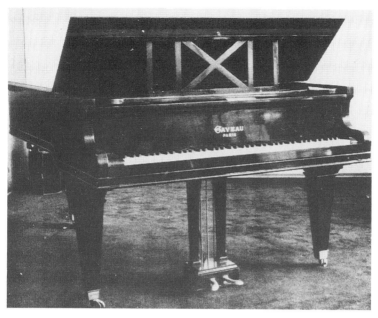

*The Gaveau piano discussed in LETTER 12, now in the Museu
Villa-Lobos in Rio de Janeiro (courtesy of the Museu Villa-Lobos)*

I beg you, as a good friend at all times, to get me out of this trouble with the Maison Gaveau, which is a terrible precipice for me.

Or else you may wire directly to Gaveau to postpone this transaction until the end of next June, at which time I shall be in Brazil and therefore have better chances to settle those 'annoying' pianos.

Personally I can ask nothing from the Maison Gaveau, because, as I said above, I would lose all my artistic prestige in Paris. This means that I am on the brink of an unforeseen precipice.

I beg you to wire me upon receipt of this letter to calm me because I am more than very worried.

On the same day on which I received your last telegram I wired to Dona Olivia and wrote an airmail letter to you, but I have had no answer as of today.

[unsigned]

The festival referred to in LETTER 12 consisted of two concerts which took place on 3 April and 7 May of that year. The first, in the Salle des Concerts Gaveau, included the *Quintetto em Forma de Chôros* for flute, oboe, clarinet, cor anglais and bassoon (composed in 1928). Its first performance had been given two weeks earlier, on 14 March 1930, in the Salle Chopin in Paris, to unfavourable reviews in the press.

When Villa-Lobos next wrote to Irving Schwerké, a few weeks after his last letter to Arnaldo Guinle, he was still under considerable pressure, this time from a heavy workload. He was, moreover, on the point of leaving Paris for Brazil.

LETTER 13
VILLA-LOBOS TO IRVING SCHWERKÉ
Original: French

Paris 9/4/930

Dear Friend

I hope you will forgive me for thanking you so late for your excellent articles but I am absolutely burdened with work, I have not even had time to sleep, one can lose one's mind.

I need not tell you how much I am touched by the interest which you show my work.

Believe in my true intellectual sympathy.

Villa-Lobos

Soon after Villa-Lobos' return to Brazil, he arranged some concerts in São Paulo. Though artistically successful they did not afford him the financial security he had enjoyed in Paris, and he expressed his dissatisfaction with life in Brazil to Arnaldo Guinle.

Manuscript first page of the Quintetto em Forma de Chôros, *to which Villa-Lobos gave this more explicitly Brazilian title only in 1930 (courtesy of Éditions Max Eschig)*

LETTER 14*
VILLA-LOBOS TO ARNALDO GUINLE
Original: Portuguese

[27 December 1930]

I can only tell you that I have calluses on my fingers from practising the cello in order to obtain the means for defending myself. I can't believe that there is at the moment someone who is more of a poor devil than I am [...,] who begs for charity and plays the mouth organ[22] so that he can live in his own country [...]. I feel ill and tired and have not had my just and deserved rewards [...]. I am not a cry-baby, even though I am the composer of the *Chôros*.[23]

But Arnaldo Guinle judged the situation differently. Political changes in Brazil, the October Revolution itself, and the provisional appointment, later confirmed, as President of Getúlio Dornelles Vargas (1883–1954)[24] caused change throughout the intellectual life of the country. Guinle, much more farsighted than the composer himself, foresaw beneficial results for Villa-Lobos from these new tendencies.

LETTER 15*
ARNALDO GUINLE TO VILLA-LOBOS
Original: Portuguese

[7 January 1931]

You have to see the situation clearly and go on fighting as you are fighting at the moment because even unforeseen things can have a beneficial effect on history, and you may find yourself on the eve of some compensation for your efforts.

---

[22] A play on words: *gaita* (mouth organ) is also a popular expression for money in the Brazilian dialect of Portuguese.

[23] Another pun: *chorar* means 'to cry'.

[24] *Cf.* pp. 43 and 49.

Guinle's premonition was to be proved correct, although Villa-Lobos still had his doubts, as his reply reveals.

LETTER 16★

VILLA-LOBOS TO ARNALDO GUINLE

Original: Portuguese

[7 February 1931]

I shall do what I can to return to Europe as quickly as possible because, as you well know, I must live in a different milieu where I can work in peace [...].

But Brazil was soon to offer Villa-Lobos possibilities he had not expected, and he was not to return to Paris until after the Second World War.

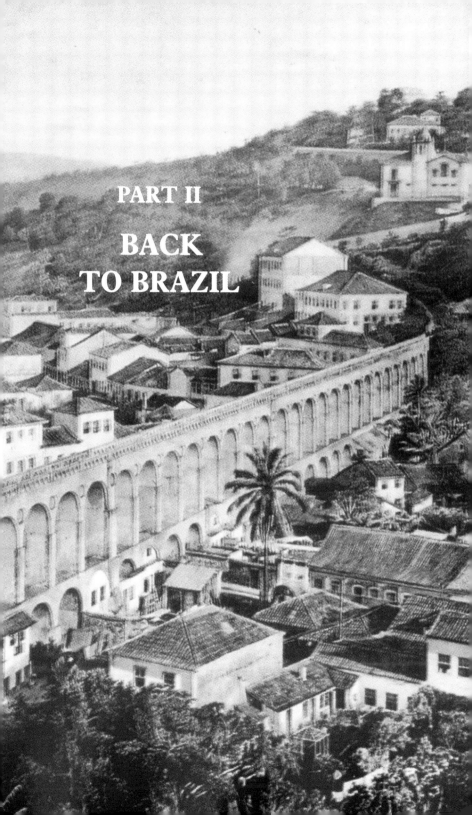

PART II

BACK
TO BRAZIL

Overleaf:
A view of part of Rio de Janeiro as Villa-Lobos would have known it
in the early years of the century

With their arrival on 1 June 1930 in Recife, in the state of Pernambuco, in the North-east of Brazil, a new era had begun for Villa-Lobos and his wife. The country to which he was returning was about to experience the October Revolution of 1930, bringing Getúlio Vargas to power; the liberal atmosphere which had prevailed until then gave way to nationalist tendencies which were to have a considerable influence on Villa-Lobos's life and career.

In the first decade of his life that can be chronicled through his letters (1927–37), Villa-Lobos' correspondence reveals two predominant emotions: a mixture of apprehension and insecurity, and strong-willed determination to achieve recognition as a composer. But his struggle to succeed was not confined to efforts on his own behalf: upon his return to Brazil he organised a series of concerts in São Paulo, presenting works he felt ought to be heard in Brazil. One of the concerts was devoted entirely to the music of Florent Schmitt (1870–1958), the French composer and critic, and a staunch admirer of Villa-Lobos – though, naturally, the concerts also featured a considerable amount of Villa-Lobos' own music.[1] Schmitt had been a critic for, first, *La Revue de France* and, later and for much longer, *Le Temps*, and he had used his position to write at length on Villa-Lobos during the Brazilian's second Paris sojourn. Since Villa-Lobos could not afford to pay for his wife to accompany him, Lucília stayed behind in Rio de Janeiro and he wrote to her there.[2] The first letter available from this exchange is undated. According to the composer's brother-in-law,[3] it dates from 1930. The loneliness he reveals in this exchange contrasts strikingly with the exuberance he manifested in person and in almost all his other extant letters; and it is interesting that, until he contracted cancer of the bladder at the age of 61, he mentioned his

---

[1] This was not the last time that Villa-Lobos was to see that Schmitt's music was heard in Brazil – *cf.* LETTERS 56 and 57, pp. 127–29.

[2] The surviving part of the exchange between Villa-Lobos and his wife appeared, in its original Portuguese, in *Villa-Lobos, Visto da Platéia e na Intimidade*, *op. cit.*, pp. 340–55. This English translation was first published in my 'Correspondence between H. Villa-Lobos and his wife Lucília', *Music & Letters*, Vol. 61, Nos. 3/4, July/October 1980, pp. 284–92.

[3] Letter from Oldemar Guimarães to me, dated 1 December 1972.

health only when he felt especially despondent, first in Paris, and
now (LETTERS 19 and 22) in Brazil.

LETTER 17
VILLA-LOBOS TO HIS WIFE
Original: Portuguese

[undated]

Luquinha
Go to the *Licêo de Artes e Officios* in the street that runs in
from the Teatro Lyrico and look for that 'mulatto' gentleman
whose name I don't remember but who organised that concert of Brazilian music I conducted two or three years ago.
Remember?

Well, find that gentleman, or someone in his place, and
ask him about an instrumentation I did for that concert of a
song by Felix Ottero, called 'A flor e a fonte'.[4] Would he
look for it and do me the great favour of lending it to me,
since I intend to perform it here in São Paulo with Bidú
Sayão[5] in honour of the composer, who very much wants to
get to know the instrumentation. See if you can manage to
bring this instrumention along with you when you come,
with the promise that it will be returned.

As far as Pery is concerned,[6] I am seeing if I can arrange a
fee of one *conto-de-reis* for him.[7] It will be difficult, though,

---

[4] Felix de Ottero (1868–1946) was a prolific composer born in the city of
Porto Alegre, in the south of Brazil; he went to Germany at an early age.
Upon his return to Brazil he settled in São Paulo, as teacher and music cri-
tic, and in 1927, together with several others, founded the Instituto de São
Paulo.

[5] In the event, the soloist was not the noted Brazilian soprano, Bidú
Sayão, but Sira Monossi. The concert programme announced the orchestral arrangement as a first performance, given by the Sociedade Sinfônica
de São Paulo at the Teatro Municipal on 24 September 1930.

[6] Pery Machado (1898–1955) was a violinist and friend of Villa-Lobos, and
occasionally played his music.

[7] *Cf.* note 19 on p. 34.

Florent Schmitt
(1870–1958)
(courtesy of
EMI France)

since the finances of the Villa-Lobos season are not very good, it seems.

I have had no news of my pianos from Arnaldo. I have just written to him to this effect.

What is being said about Luiz[8] is so much posturing and pretence, because I know that I am fully entitled to a refund of these 'crooked' duties I paid to the Customs.

It's very cold here, so when you come put on warm clothes.

Nothing else, kisses and greetings

from your Villa.

PS: On presentation of this chit you will receive at the Rio branch of this bank the sum of 500 *milreis*. You can expect a communication from the bank.

from your Villa.

---

[8] 'Luiz' has not been identified. According to the Guimarães family, he was connected with the Guinles.

The Teatro Lyrico (courtesy of the Biblioteca Nacional,
Rio de Janeiro)

LETTER 18
VILLA-LOBOS TO HIS WIFE
Original: Portuguese

S. Paulo, 15/7/930

My Lucas

I sent you 500 *milreis* to cover your present requirements and to pay for your journey to S. Paulo when the time comes. Simply let me know the day when you will be arriving, and I'll meet you at the station.

If by chance, this is not enough, let me know right away, and I will send more, at whatever sacrifice.

The concert of the 12th went well, though it could have been better if I had had more rehearsal.

The second [concert] has been fixed for the 26th of this month and the 3rd for the 30th or 31st.[9]

I think you will find me very slim, for I eat almost nothing and work like a madman.

I don't know when I can manage to get some rest.

---

[9] The concerts took place on dates slightly different from those Villa-Lobos had anticipated. They were eventually scheduled for 28 July and 11, 25 and 31 August. Two more concerts were to come, on 24 and 30 September, the second under the auspices of the Cultura Artistica in São Paulo.

I think it would be as well for you to get here only at the end of the month because by then I shall have more money and be able to cope with our expenses at the hotel here, which will be 50 *milreis* a day.

When you come to the concerts I am conducting, the best programmes will be those in August and September.

Regarding our chamber music concerts, I am awaiting final arrangements from various impresarios here. When you come, bring the two orch. batons I left behind.

Nothing else, kisses and greetings to Mama and lots more for you.

from your Villa

LETTER 19
VILLA-LOBOS TO HIS WIFE
Original: Portuguese

S. Paulo, 17/7/930

Lucas

The day before yesterday I sent you 500 *milreis* through the Banco Nordeste de S. Paulo and went to the Post Office myself to mail you a long letter.

I now write in response to your letter which I have just received, in which you tell me about a radio festival with Newton.[10]

I really don't want you to take part in any concert without earning at least 200 *milreis* or so.

If they want to put on some festival, they should do it on their own, for I *will not countenance the use of any of my works in Rio* except on payment of a fee. I am tired of 'mockery' and injustices, and for me Rio is already artistically dead. Nothing . . . Nothing and Nothing!

I want you to pack your bags and come to me, where you belong.

Newton, whom as you know very well I value as an excellent friend and committed artist, will forgive me this protest;

[10] Newton de Menezes Pádua (1894–1966), cellist, friend of Villa-Lobos and interpreter of his music.

*Map of Brazil, showing in capital letters the places mentioned
in Villa-Lobos' letters (drawn by Patricia Hatch)*

Villa-Lobos with President Getúlio Vargas (1883–1954) in 1950, at a reception in the Ministry of Foreign Affairs in Rio de Janeiro, then the capital of Brazil; second from right is Arminda Villa-Lobos (courtesy of the Museu Villa-Lobos)

for, even with due regard to him, I want to hear no more of concerts in Rio unless they pay us as if we were good foreigners.

So don't write to me any more in these terms. And if you do take part, only for a minimum of 200 *milreis*.

As for your complaint about my not having written more often, that is unfair, for I have already written to you five times, and you know very well that I hate writing letters.

I have had a letter from Pery which I will answer as soon as I can. Another from our 'concierge de Paris' telling us that all is well.

Here everybody is waiting for you so that they can fête us jointly. Souza Lima,[11] Fonseca,[12] D. Olivia,[13] Baby de Guilherme,[14] who ask after you all the time – and others.

[11] João de Souza Lima (1898–1982), Brazilian pianist, composer and conductor.

[12] Unidentified; possibly a friend of Villa-Lobos.

[13] *Cf.* note 18 on p. 34.

[14] Wife of Guilherme de Andrade e Almeida (1890–1969), Brazilian poet, essayist and journalist.

You need only let me know for certain which Cruzeiro[15] train you will be taking – for, unless I am mistaken, you will be visiting Bilita[16] first – and I can meet you at the station.

I have been ill, I don't know what with. I have lost weight to the extent that everyone notices, and I feel exhausted and despondent, although I am always surrounded by admirers and made much of. I can't account for my present state of physical decline.

Perhaps I am worn out by my constant protests against the endless injustices that I have suffered lately.

Oh! How I wish I could overcome everything and flee to 'hell'!

In short, my problem is calmness and perseverance.

The 1st symph. concert [12 July] was so-so, and I am rehearsing everyday for the 2nd concert which will be perhaps on the 26th of this month. I hope you will be here by then.

Nothing else, a thousand kisses to our beloved Grandma, and more to you and greetings.

From your Villa

Two years passed before Villa-Lobos again had occasion to write to Lucília. The financial security he required to support himself and his wife had now come his way: on 18 April 1932, by a government decree, the Superintendência de Educação Musical e Artística (SEMA) was established;[17] it made the teaching of choral singing in schools compulsory. Villa-Lobos was appointed its head, a post created especially for him.

The position not only provided him with a fixed income for the first time in his life but also confronted him with a host of educational tasks completely new to him. The people he now met in his daily tasks were not musicians and other artists but largely government officials, school teachers, their pupils. Most of these people came from a different background from Villa-Lobos, had

---

[15] Brazilian railway company.

[16] Pet name of Villa-Lobos' sister Carmen (1888–1970), married to Danton Condorcet da Silva Jardim.

[17] *Cf. Presença de Villa-Lobos*, Museu Villa-Lobos, Rio de Janeiro, Vol. 10 (1977), p. 31.

not had the same kind of education, and did not move in the artistic circles that were familiar to him. But he was an adaptable person; moreover, he had the support of his wife, herself a musician (Lucília was a pianist and teacher, and often performed her husband's music), at least during the first six years of his new life.

His new position meant that he now had regular office hours and travelled less; as a result he had less reason to write to his wife, and his letters, often just short notes, usually tell of concerts outside Rio. The job also brought with it influence and self-assurance, both mirrored in the next letters he wrote to Lucília – although his health still presents a cause for concern.

LETTER 20
VILLA-LOBOS TO HIS WIFE
Original: Portuguese

Rio, 5/5/932

Lucília

Today Dr Pedro Ernesto[18] signed your appointment as a teacher in one of the Technical Secondary Schools, which establishes the right of assigning you to the Orsina da Fonseca School, as you and the headmistress there both want.

Also the Minister of Education is appointing you under contract at the Ginásio [secondary school] Pedro II, according to a telegram which I am sending you along with another sent to me by the Minister himself. I have thanked all concerned by telegram.

You can be confident that they can wait a month for you with these appointments, which will bring you a further 1,750 *milreis*.

So it is best for you to stay on as long as you can so as to be really strong when you come, because you will have a lot of work to do. (My mother has today sent you 200 *milreis* by post.)

I shall be sending you in the coming ten to fifteen days a

[18] Pedro Ernesto do Rego Batista (1886–1942) was 'Federal Interventor' (governor by appointment) of what was then the Federal District (i.e., the city, not the state, of Rio de Janeiro) and later its mayor.

The Teatro João Caetano, where many of Villa-Lobos' SEMA concerts were given (courtesy of the Biblioteca Nacional, Rio de Janeiro)

further 200 *milreis* for your fare, and if you need any more, let me know in time.

You can arrive here at the end of this month or the start of next, because I am tying up the whole business of your appointment, and only your signature is necessary to bring it to a conclusion, which could be a month from today.

I think it is best for you to write two letters, one to Mme Anísio Teixeira[19] and another to Dr Roxo.[20]

No more for now. All is well.

Villa

[19] Anísio Spinola Teixeira (1900–71) was, in 1932, director of the Department of Education.

[20] Unidentified.

*The Instituto de Educação, another venue for Villa-Lobos' SEMA
concerts (courtesy of the Biblioteca Nacional, Rio de Janeiro)*

LETTER 21
VILLA-LOBOS TO HIS WIFE AND HIS MOTHER
Original: Portuguese

Baia, 4/7/934

Lucília
I stopped in Baia to catch a flight to Recife tomorrow. Until
now I am doing fine.
Greetings to everybody and thinking of my mother.

Villa

My Mother
I did well so far

Your son Villa (Tuhu)

*Anísio Spinola
Teixeira
(1890–1971),
Director of the
Department of
Education in 1932
and therefore Villa-
Lobos' superior
(courtesy of the
Biblioteca
Nacional, Rio de
Janeiro)*

LETTER 22
VILLA-LOBOS TO HIS WIFE
Original: Portuguese

Recife 9/7/34

Lucília

Here everything has gone well, apart from my stomach. I
have done everything possible to improve my digestion, but a
palpitation on my left side [is] thoroughly unwelcome. I was
afraid of travelling by air because of this, but I decided that a

journey by air is much less upsetting than one by sea or land. So I am returning by plane and think I shall be leaving here on the 16th or 17th, on a Panair or Condor sea plane, and will be two days travelling. I cannot say which day for certain, because my work here is not yet finished and I am very busy with speeches, interviews, giving audiences, lectures and etc. I think we shall be going in a party that is thoroughly artistic, educational and official to visit the states of Paraíba and Rio Grande do Norte.

We shall travel in a number of official cars.

I shall of course find it extremely hard going; still no matter, there will surely come an end to my involvement in this peregrination.

Please don't say anything to my people about my health.

Are you in office at the [Ginásio] Pedro II now?

Have you received your salary from the city hall?

Have they sent you 800 *milreis* from SEMA?

You can reply to me by airmail when you receive this, to the following address, and I shall still receive it in time.

Pensão Palácio

Rua Concordia 148

Recife-Pernambuco

My thoughts and greetings to my mother, Candonguinha[21] and to you.

From Villa

PS: A letter is in the post with cuttings and reports from the newspapers here.

Villa

In April 1936 Villa-Lobos left Rio de Janeiro for Prague, to attend the First International Congress for Musical Education,

---

[21] Pet name (diminutive of *candonga*, 'darling') of Villa-Lobos' niece and godchild, Laiseni, daughter of Luiz Guimarães, Villa-Lobos' brother-in-law (letter to me from Oldemar Guimarães, dated 27 November 1978).

sponsored by Leo Kestenberg.[22] By that time his relationship with his wife had deteriorated markedly, for reasons that are at present unknown, and may well remain so. He and Lucília had lived at 10 Rua Didimo in Rio de Janeiro since 1919 – but Villa-Lobos never returned there after his trip to Europe. He informed his wife of his decision to separate from her in a guarded letter, written in Berlin on his way back from Prague. They had been married for a little over 22 years.

LETTER 23
VILLA-LOBOS TO HIS WIFE
Original: Portuguese

Berlin, 28–5–36

Lucília

This three-month trip of mine to Europe was undertaken especially to decide my personal life, once and for all, and not really to fulfil my obligations as a delegate to the International Congress for Musical Education.

I am sure that you will not be at all surprised by the decisive news that follows below.

For a long time I have been reflecting on this resolution.

The reasons are few but just.

I cannot live in the company of someone from whom I feel entirely estranged, isolated, [by whom I feel] constricted, in short without any affection save for a certain gratitude at your faithfulness during many years in my company.

I proclaim our absolute freedom. I do so, however, with a quiet conscience, in the knowledge that I have done everything to ensure that you lack nothing. It was entirely through my own efforts that I secured for you the excellent positions you now hold, as a result of which you earn more than I do and have better prospects.

---

22 Kestenberg (1882–1962) was Hungarian-born and finished his career prominent in the musical life of Israel, having been ousted by the Nazis, first from Berlin in 1933 and then from Prague in 1938. He was a fine pianist, studying in Berlin with Busoni.

My wish is that you will never feel any rancour towards me
or anyone else, but to accept with calm and resignation that
our situation could not end in any other way than this.

Hence, when I return I shall not come back to our home at
10 Rua Didimo, which I regard as being henceforth entirely
your responsibility.

Naturally, I must accept responsibility for all the expenses
that result from this change in our lives.

I will send a reliable person to fetch my personal
belongings, and I will live alone with my mother. Wishing
you much happiness in your new life,

Villa-Lobos

LUCÍLIA VILLA-LOBOS TO HER HUSBAND
Original: Portuguese

14–6–1936

Villa

I received your letter of 28 May, but did not reply at once
because I did not know where to write, seeing that you were
on your way back here, and so I am replying now. It is
unnecessary for me to comment on the fact of your outrageous and absurd decision, but I am bound to point out that I
am your legal wife, that you undertook responsibilities towards me, and that you owe me personal satisfaction. I do
not speak of your duties towards society, above all as regards
the position you occupy in it as one concerned with education, because this I leave to your own conscience to direct
you. Much as I read your letter and try to draw deductions to
lead me to a conclusion on the motives that have led you to
this decision, I find no point of departure to set me in the
right direction, unless it is that the last trace of feeling for me
on your part has disappeared. You say that, when you agreed
to go to Europe, it was with the aim of taking the opportunity of following a new course with regard to our life. This
does not seem very probable to me, because, in that case, the

One of the Panair seaplanes in use at the time of Villa-Lobos' travels in 1934 (courtesy of Pan American World Airways, New York, of which the now defunct Brazilian Panair was a subsidiary)

cards you wrote to me earlier would make no sense. You also said that all you recognised as a common bond in my life with you was my faithfulness, and as regards that, I take pride in telling you that I owe you no debt on that score. If latterly I have not shared your joys and sorrows, it is simply due to the fact that you have given me no opportunity to do so, since I do not even know what I have meant to you. This letter does not contain an appeal to you to return, because I cannot tell how far your animosity towards me has gone. Meanwhile, it is my pleasure and duty to tell you that, so long as you do not give me the satisfaction to which I am entitled, I continue as before in my place, waiting for you. But you should know that I have not even the slightest idea of putting pressure on you to return to our home, but simply desire that you should, as I do not see any reasons that you

The airship LZ 127, 'Graf Zeppelin', in which Villa-Lobos travelled to Europe in 1936. The first non-stop crossing of the South Atlantic by Zeppelin was on 8 May 1930, from Seville to Recife. On 20 March 1932 a regular Zeppelin service between Friedrichshafen and Recife was begun, with Lufthansa planes making short feeder flights in Germany to shorten airmail delivery times (courtesy of Lufthansa)

should do otherwise. As regards your remarks to the effect that what I am I owe to you, I accept that as true, and if my gratitude is what you want, this [letter] brings it to you, though I take the opportunity of reminding you that this could not have been otherwise since, in a situation involving husband and wife, my co-operation could not but play its part. And so, Villa, I am ready to submit myself to God's will, but for the satisfaction at least of my own conscience I shall continue to wait to hear your reasons or to await your final word.

Lucília

Villa-Lobos in 1935
(courtesy of the
Museu Villa-Lobos)

Lucília's last known letter to her husband was clearly written in response to his answer – now apparently lost[23] – to her letter of 14 June.

LETTER 25
LUCÍLIA VILLA-LOBOS TO HER HUSBAND
Original: Portuguese

19–6–936

Villa

Your last letter has caused me surprise and very great offence.

I never imagined that, open and impulsive as you admit you are, and enjoying *absolute liberty*, you would endeavour to hide the real reason for your conduct, casting around for

---

[23] Letter from Oldemar Guimarães to me, dated 27 November 1978.

*Lucília Guimarães
Villa-Lobos
(1886–1966) at the
age of 45
(photographed
by N. Fiorini; courtesy
of Oldemar
Guimarães)*

excuses which are in any case quite unjust and without foundation for a decision as serious as our final separation.

I cannot in the least accept your allegations. Nor can I stay silent in the face of a charge as serious and utterly untrue as that I am accused of. It is unbelievable that you should have lived with me for 22-and-a-half years, knowing my shy temperament and stable character, and now be capable of listening to such base and outrageous insinuations. I am astonished above all that you should never have said a word to me about the matter and did not make the slightest reference to it in your letter from Berlin, despite the fact that now you have judged it 'extremely serious' and *latterly* a matter of observation.

My attitude has always been one and the same and known to all – to be your sincere companion and collaborator. If the many enemies you have have been busy spreading this *infamous nonsense*, surely your work, your response, your compositions have by themselves crushed any such outrageous allegation.

The proofs I have given to the contrary are countless and

Antônio de Sá Pereira (1888–1966), the Brazilian composer and teacher in whose company Villa-Lobos travelled to Europe (courtesy of the Biblioteca Nacional, Rio de Janeiro)

you would see them well enough if your present pride and obsession did not prevent you. And despite the humiliations I have suffered, I continue encouraging interest in your work and making it known in every post I hold, even though you are not there to see it.

My devotion and sincerity have now grown less. I regard Villa the man and Villa the artist as quite distinct. I think, in any case, despite your insisting in your decision not to return home, that it would be better for us to have, as I already asked, a personal understanding. Meanwhile, our situation, should you not respond to this request, will be what you have made it, since all that interests me is that you return of your own free will, if there is any affection still on your part.

My attitude will not be one of hostility but of all possible loyalty and discretion, as I am already proving by entrusting

Pedro Ernesto do Rego Batista (1886–1942) 'Federal Interventor' (governor by appointment) of the Federal District (i.e., the city of Rio de Janeiro); he was responsible for Lucília Villa-Lobos' appointment to a teaching post (courtesy of the Biblioteca Nacional, Rio de Janeiro)

my own brother, someone in my confidence, with the delivery of this letter.

You should quite clearly understand, however, that I will not relinquish any of my legal rights as your wife and shall continue to sign myself Lucília Guimarães Villa-Lobos. This I must emphasise, as I cannot but mention the offence your present attitude caused me, addressing the reply your *chauffeur* brought me to 'Lucília Guimarães V.L.' – a form of address I compared with those on the cards you sent me from Europe ('Lucília Villa-Lobos') when you had not yet got to the point of charging me with this 'infamous nonsense'.

[unsigned]

Thereafter Villa-Lobos and his wife went their separate ways, Lucília (who died in 1966) surviving him by six-and-a-half years. The person who was to share the remaining 23-and-a-half years of his life he found in Arminda Neves d'Almeida. She was a pupil of Villa-Lobos (and 25 years younger than him) and became *de facto*, though not *de iure*, his second wife: they never married, since divorce was not permitted in Brazil until 1977, although she later acquired his name by deed-poll.

Villa-Lobos' position at SEMA lasted until November 1943, when he was appointed Director of the Conservatório de Canto Orfeônico in Rio.[24] Only one other letter appears to have survived from this period of nearly twelve years. It is addressed to Laurinda Santos Lobo,[25] at whose house Villa-Lobos had been a frequent guest in the 1920s. She had helped him financially at that time, and also later in Paris, when he required funds in addition to those sent him by the Guinle brothers. Villa-Lobos expressed his gratitude by dedicating to her his *Quatuor* for harp, celesta, flute and alto saxophone with women's voices; it was premiered on 21 October 1921 in a concert dedicated to her, given in the Salão Nobre of the *Jornal do Comércio* in Rio de Janeiro.

Villa-Lobos' position at SEMA also involved the organising of symphonic and choral concerts, for which task he sought Laurinda Santos Lobo's help. The concerts were held either in the Teatro Municipal, the Teatro João Caetano (formerly known as the Teatro São Pedro de Alcântara), or the Instituto de Educação, all in Rio de Janeiro. But in 1937 Villa-Lobos was no longer the petitioner of the '20s, as the tone of LETTER 26 shows.[26] As head of a municipal department, he commanded authority and was in a position to enlist prominent citizens to support his plans for a 'National Art' in accordance with the nationalist ideas of the Vargas regime. Villa-Lobos' energy and penchant for the colossal were enlisted to organise mass choral and orchestral concerts, especially on Brazil's Independence Day (7 September), with between 10,000 and 35,000 school children singing patriotic songs; these Villa-Lobos would conduct from an elevated platform, dressed in flaming colours, in open-air stadia, in the presence of government officials and large numbers of citizens.

---

[24] It trained teachers in the instruction of schoolchildren in choral singing. When this discipline was no longer part of the national curriculum, the Conservatório adopted the name Instituto Villa-Lobos; it thereafter became the Centro do Arte and has been incorporated into the University of Rio de Janeiro.

[25] *Cf.* note 5 on p. 22.

[26] *Cf.* my 'The Paris Bibliothèque Nationale's Autograph Letter of Villa-Lobos to His Sponsor', *The Journal of Musicological Research*, Vol. 3, Nos. 3/4, 1981, pp. 423–33.

LETTER 26
VILLA-LOBOS TO LAURINDA SANTOS LOBO
Original: Portuguese

Department of Education

Origin:

Federal District,   [date left blank] 1937

Unforgettable friend

In the happy fight for civic-artistic education in our Brazil, the names of D. Laurinda Santos Lobo and D. Olivia Guedes Penteado[27] could not but be always remembered as genuine supporters of National Art.

From this moment, my esteemed friend is elected as commander-in-chief of the illustrious social army of our best Rio de Janeiro elite, in order to enlist subscribers for the Cultural Symphony Concerts at popular prices, to take place at the M[unicipal] Theatre next October.

I enclose some programmes to facilitate the propaganda and send my infinite respects and eternal admiration for my esteemed friend and all those who are dear to her.

Villa-Lobos

With the outbreak of World War II Villa-Lobos' correspondence turned to the United States and, later, as communications permitted, also to Europe. The close economic and cultural ties between Brazil and the United States contributed in large measure to the growing fame Villa-Lobos enjoyed in North America. As a result he began to receive requests for information about himself and his music. One early letter came from the American composer

---

[27] *Cf.* note 18 on p. 34.

TEATRO MUNICIPAL

(ENTRADA FRANCA)

CONCERTO CULTURAL POPULAR DO *ORFEAO DE PROFESSORES* do
Distrito Federal organizado pela SEMA (Superintendencia de Educação Musical e
Artistica do Departamento de Educação).
Sob a regencia do *Maestro Villa-Lobos*

SABADO, 18 DE DEZEMBRO DE 1937, ÁS 20½ HORAS

1.ª PARTE

(Classico)

a) Preludio n.º 22 (x) (Sem palavras) — Côro mixto a capela *J. S. Bach*
1 b) Preludio n.º 14 (x) (Sem palavras) — Côro mixto a capela " " "
c) Fuga n.º 21 (x) (Sem palavras) — Côro mixto a capela.. " " "

(Romantico)

a) Reverie (x) — Côro mixto a capela — (Vocalismo) ...... *Schumann*
b) Serenata (x) — Côro mixto a capela — (Vocalismo) ...... *Schubert*
Letra de X X X
2 c) Ay-Ay-Ay (x) — Côro mixto a capela .... *Popular Chileno*
Letra — popular traduzida
d) Lamento (x) — (Sem palavras) — Côro mixto a capela... *Homero Barreto*
e) Iphigenia en Aulide (x) — Opera antiga — C. mixto a capela *Gluck*

2.ª PARTE

(Folclóre infantil antigo, ambientedo)

a) Manquinha (x) — 1.ª audição .... *Folclóre Brasileiro*
Letra anonima
3 b) O Gato (x) — 1.ª audição .... " "
Letra anonima
c) Você diz que sabe tudo (x) — 1.ª adição .... " "
Letra anonima

a) Casinha pequenina (Folclóre ambientado) .... *L. Fernandez*
Letra — Guimarães Passos
4 b) Jupira — Opera Nacional (côro interno) .... *Francisco Braga*
c) O Ferreiro — Original .... *Barrozo Netto*
Letra — Paulo Gustavo

a) Jaquibau (Folclóre ambientado) .... *H. Villa-Lobos*
Letra anonima
b) Bazzum — (Original) .... " " "
Letra — Domingos Magarinos
c) Patria — (Civico-artistico) .... " " "
Letra — P. Haroldo

(x) arranjo de H. V. L.

Programme of one of Villa-Lobos' 'Cultural Symphony Concerts'

*Caricature of
Laurinda Santos
Lobo (courtesy of the
Biblioteca
Nacional, Rio de
Janeiro)*

Frederick Jacobi.[28] Although documentation has been difficult to find, LETTER 27 seems to suggest that Jacobi had expressed interest in arranging performances of some of Villa-Lobos' music; I have been unable to ascertain whether any performances came about as a result.

[28] Jacobi (1891–1952) studied composition with Rubin Goldmark and Ernest Bloch. He taught at the Juilliard School of Music (1936–50) and also at Berkeley and Mills College. He served on the board of directors of the American section of the ISCM and on the executive board of the League of Composers; he was an active promoter of music by living composers and a frequent contributor of articles and reviews to *Modern Music*. His compositions include an opera and a variety of orchestral, choral, chamber and piano music.

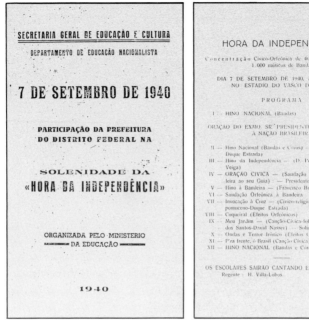

Programme of Independence Day celebrations, 1940

LETTER 27
VILLA-LOBOS TO FREDERICK JACOBI
Original: French

Rio de Janeiro, 12 February 1940

Dear Mr. Frederick Jacobi:

I have the pleasure to reply to you and thank you for the attention you are kindly giving me.

As for chamber-music works you can choose from the catalogue which I enclose herewith. You can obtain them in New-York from the representative of the House Max-Eschig (Associated Published Musicpublishers Incorporation – C/o G. Ricordi – & C. 12 West 45th Street).

*The American
composer and writer
Frederick Jacobi
(1891–1952)
(courtesy of the
Juilliard School of
Music, New York)*

Allow me to take this opportunity to send you also some explanatory notes about my works and my biography.

Looking forward to hearing from you,

Sincerely yours

H. Villa-Lobos
Director of the Music Department

Av. Almirante Barroso, 81
5º andar-sala 504 [fifth floor – room 504]
Rio de Janeiro-Brasil

In 1940 Villa-Lobos was visited in Rio de Janeiro by the Russian-born American lexicographer, Nicolas Slonimsky, then writing

```
                          Rio de Janeiro, le 12 Février 1940.



                   Cher Monsieur Frederick Jacobi

                   J'ai le plaisir de vous répondre en vous
             remerciant l'attention que vous voulez bien m'accor-
             der.
                   Quant aux musiques de chambre vous pouvez
             choisir dans le catalogue de  mes oeuvres que je vous
             remets ci-joint. Vous pourrez les obtenir à New-York
             avec le représentant de la Maison Max-Eschig (Associa
             ted Published Musicpublishers Incorporation- C/o G.
             Ricordi - & C.12 Weast 45 th Street).
                   Permetez-moi de profiter cette occasion
             pour vous envoyer aussi quelques notes explicatives
             sur mes oeuvres et ma biographie.
                   Au plaisir de vous lire, je vous prie de
             croire,Cher Monsieur, à l'assurance de mes sentiments
             les plus distingués,
                                      H.Villa-Lobos

                                      Directeur du Département de Mu-
             Av.Almirante Barroso,81                sique
                 52 andar-sala 504
                 Rio de Janeiro-Brasil
```

Letter (27) *to Frederick Jacobi* (*courtesy of the Music Division,*
New York Public Library)

articles for *The Christian Science Monitor* in Boston.[29] The purpose
of the visit was the acquisition of information about Villa-Lobos
and his music, not least the dates of first performances, for a book

[29] Slonimsky's varied career as pianist, composer, conductor, writer and
lexicographer began soon after his birth in 1894, in St Petersburg. His
witty and erudite autobiography, *Perfect Pitch* (in his words, a 'rueful
autopsy') appeared in 1988 (Oxford University Press, New York and
Oxford).

*Nicolas Slonimsky
(b. 1894), on his
travels to research
his* Music of Latin
America *(courtesy of
Nicolas Slonimsky)*

Slonimsky was researching; it was published as *Music of Latin America*.[30]

LETTER 28
VILLA-LOBOS TO NICOLAS SLONIMSKY
Original: French

Rio de Janeiro, 29 April 1940

Dear Mr Slonimsky

I have received your letter of 2 April which I reply with pleasure by sending you herewith enclosed my photograph and the explanatory notes about my work.

As to the music which you have requested, I shall send it soon. I look forward to hearing from you.

Sincerely yours
H. Villa-Lobos

Av. Almte. Barroso, 81 – Edif. Andorinha – 5º and. s/504, Rio de janeiro – Brazil

[30] Thomas Y. Crowell, New York, 1945; reprinted by Da Capo Press, New York, 1972.

LETTER 29
VILLA-LOBOS TO NICOLAS SLONIMSKY
Original: French

Rio, 6 February, 1941

Dear Mr Nicolas Slonimsky

Having received your letter only at the end of last year, upon my return from a trip to Buenos Aires, I reply with apologies for the long delay.

I infinitely regret that I cannot comply with your request regarding Chôros No. 5, because it belongs to Maison Max Eschig. Concerning the first performance dates of my works, it is impossible for me to give you any information since I have not catalogued them.

I am sending you, enclosed, my biography, the catalogue of my works and some explanatory notes about them.

I look forward to hearing from you.

Sincerely yours
H. Villa-Lobos

Programme of concert Villa-Lobos conducted in Buenos Aires, alluded to LETTER 29.

PART III

**NORTH AMERICA
AND CONDUCTING**

Overleaf:
The Main Building (now the Jefferson Building) of the Library of
Congress at the time of Villa-Lobos' contacts with it (courtesy of the
Library of Congress)

A new period began in Villa-Lobos' life in 1944: his entry onto the North American scene with guest appearances as composer-conductor. This led to unexpected recognition, even fame; indeed, from then on he was to visit North America every year until his death in 1959.

Negotiations with concert agents, organisations and orchestras had been underway for some time, as is revealed in LETTER 30 to Serge Koussevitzky, an old friend from his days in Paris.

LETTER 30

VILLA-LOBOS TO SERGE KOUSSEVITZKY

Original: French

M.E.H. National Conservatory of Orpheonic Singing
Avenida Pasteur 350, Praia Vermelha

Rio de Janeiro, 24 May 1944

Mr. Sèrge Koussevitzky

Dear Friend

We have not met for a long time since the good times in Paris. Paris, alas!

Nonetheless, I always remember your admirable triumphs as a great conductor. So well that on the occasion of the twentieth anniversary of your artistic career in the United States, I invited some colleagues of mine who had joined me in the fight to raise the universal artistic level, to send you a cable of congratulations, which was done with immense pleasure.

I take advantage of this opportunity to let you know that this time it will soon be possible for me to take off some time from my unbelievable official activities in my country and that I wish to spend some months in the various artistic centres abroad, as I should now be able.

75

Having received, for many years, invitations from some American countries and several cities in the United States to conduct festivals of my works, I can now accept them, as I should have liked to earlier. Nonetheless,[1] I have written to everybody who invited me suggesting the schedule of concerts in the following order:

– *In September* (second *fortnight*): Montevidéu, Buenos Aires and Chile
– *From October to December:* Panama, Mexico and Canada
– *December 1944 to January 1945:* New York, Chicago, Illinois and Los Angeles
– *January to February 1945:* Philadelphia and Boston

I am still waiting for an urgent answer to fix the dates, deal with the conditions and arrangement for the official air tickets, if possible.

With this schedule, I venture to ask you if you would like your admirable orchestra in Boston to play, under my direction, a concert with premieres of my works in the following programme:

Bachianas Brasileiras No. 7 – (25 minutos)[2]
3rd Suite do Descobrimento do Brasil – (idem)[3]
Chôros No. 6 – (idem)[4]
Rudepoêma – (30 minutos)[5]

Considering the extraordinary technical and artistic value of your orchestra I believe five full rehearsals and one for the

---

[1] Villa-Lobos' French reads 'Pourtant'; he obviously means 'Donc' ('Therefore').

[2] The seventh of the *Bachianas Brasileiras* (1942) is dedicated to Gustavo Capanema, then Minister of Education, to whom Villa-Lobos was responsible in his own educational work.

[3] Villa-Lobos arranged a total of four suites from his music to the 1937 film *The Discovery of Brazil*.

[4] *Chôros* No. 6 is scored for full orchestra. Villa-Lobos began to compose it in 1926, but finished it only shortly before its premiere in 1942.

[5] Villa-Lobos' orchestration (1932) of the piano original of 1921–26, composed for Arthur Rubinstein.

Villa-Lobos at the age of 53, in a photograph inscribed 'to the Teatro Colón in Buenos Aires with all the gratitude of Villa-Lobos' (courtesy of the Museu Villa-Lobos)

percussion alone will be sufficient.

As for expenses, I shall ask only for the tickets, accommodation for two persons and the royalties for hire and performance.

Moreover, I shall be extremely honoured if my dear friend could be made interested to include in his repertoire some other of my symphonic works which are still unknown to him.

What do you say to all this? – Would it be possible?

Looking forward to hearing from you, I am your friend and admirer

always your

Villa-Lobos

In the event, Villa-Lobos' debut in the United States was on 26 November 1944, with the Janssen Symphony Orchestra in Los Angeles. His programme featured the Second Symphony, Sixth *Chôros* and *Rudepoêma*, and although the concert itself was not too well received he was feted as a true celebrity; among the honours he received was an honorary doctorate in law from Occidental College. Koussevitzky was to accord Villa-Lobos the opportunity of conducting the Boston Symphony Orchestra, though in a programme slightly different from that which the composer had suggested.[6]

In 1945 Harold Spivacke (1904–77), Chief of the Music Division of the Library of Congress in Washington DC, commissioned Villa-Lobos, on behalf of the Elizabeth Sprague Coolidge Foundation, to write a composition; two cables and one letter of Villa-Lobos refer to it. The work, a Trio for violin, viola and cello, was premiered by the Albeneri Trio at the Founder's Day Concert on 30 October 1945, in the Coolidge Auditorium at the Library of Congress.

Villa-Lobos' first cable to Spivacke was received on 17 August 1945, according to The Library of Congress:

AGREE WILL SEND STRING TRIO BEFORE FIRST OCTOBER
CORDIALLY

VILLA-LOBOS

The second cable arrived on 8 October:

SENDING NOW SCORE TRIO AIRMAIL FOLLOW NEXT
AIRMAIL INSTRUMENTAL PARTS CORDIALLY

VILLA-LOBOS

---

[6] The concert, in the Sanders Theatre of Harvard University, consisted of two movements (the 'Toccata' and 'Fugue') from *Bachianas Brasileiras* No. 7, the first performance of the *Chôros* No. 12 and, after the interval, *Rudepoêma*.

Manuscript first page of Villa-Lobos' String Trio
(courtesy of Éditions Max Eschig)

Harold Spivacke (1904–77) with Elizabeth Sprague Coolidge
(1864–1953), the American patroness of the arts who, in 1925,
established the Elizabeth Sprague Coolidge Foundation at the Library
of Congress (courtesy of Library of Congress, Washington DC)

LETTER 31
VILLA-LOBOS TO HAROLD SPIVACKE
Original: English

Ministry of Education and Health
National Conservatory of Orpheonic Singing
Avenida Pasteur 350 (Urca). – Rio de Janeiro

October 12, – 1945

Mr HAROLD SPIVACKE
Chief, Music Division
The Library of Congress
Washington, D.C. – U.S.A.

My dear Mr. Harold Spivacke:

I am writing to confirm you my wire of 6th current in which it was announced the sending of the Trio's score and instrumental parts which I composed for the Coolidge Foundation. – The score has been sent already by airmail addressed to Mr. Henri Leiser[7] of the William Morris Agency, Inc. (113 West 57th Street, Steinway Hall, New York, 19, – N.Y.) who will set it up to you. – The parts follow today, also by airmail and addressed to you directly.

Expecting a word on the receiving of that music and expressing you my best wishes, I am

cordially yours
(H. Villa-Lobos)

In the spring of the following year, 1946, Villa-Lobos turned again to Koussevitzky to try to place a young Brazilian conductor, Eleazar de Carvalho (born 1912), with Koussevitzky's students' orchestra at Tanglewood, the summer home of the Boston Symphony Orchestra at Lenox, Massachusetts.

LETTER 32
VILLA-LOBOS TO SERGE KOUSSEVITZKY
Original: English

Ministry of Education and Health
National Department of Education
National Conservatory of Orpheonic Singing
Avenida Pasteur, 350 (Urca). – Rio de Janeiro. – Brazil

May 13th, 1946

Master SERGE KOUSSEVITZKY
U.S.A. – (*By hand*)

My dear friend:

I have the pleasure of introducing and recommending to you my countryman and friend ELEAZAR DE CAR-VALHO, young musician who has much talent for orchestral conducting.

---

[7] Henri Leiser (1899–1973) was Villa-Lobos' concert agent at the time.

He is in the U.S. especially to perfect himself in such a difficult art and no one better than you, egregious Master, to give him efficient orientation with so precious counsels based in so great experience.

Very grateful for the consideration which you would give to these lines, have an affectionated embracing from the friend and admiror who wishes you, as ever, all happiness,

(Villa-Lobos)

As Koussevitzky had not responded to Villa-Lobos' previous hand-delivered message, he cabled to Tanglewood on 4 July 1946:

PRAY FAVOUR BEST WAY POSSIBLE PRETENSIONS
ELEAZAR CARVALHO YOUR CONDUCTING COURSE

VILLA-LOBOS

Koussevitzky cabled back the following day:

CARVALJO ALREADY JOINED MY COURSES
CONDUCTING STUDENTS ORCHESTRA SPLENDIDLY

GREETINGS SERGE KOUSSEVITZKY

This episode was concluded with a last, undated, letter from Villa-Lobos.

LETTER 33
VILLA-LOBOS TO SERGE KOUSSEVITZKY
Original: English

Ministry of Education and Health
National Conservatory of Orpheonic Singing
Avenida Pasteur, 350 (Urca). – Rio de Janeiro, Brasil

Master SERGE KOUSSEVITZKY

– Tangle Wood Lenox
Massachusetts. – U.S.A.

Illustrious and dear Friend:

It was with greatest satisfaction that I received your cable communicating the so happy result of my request in favour of Eleazar de Carvalho, youngman of real talent for conducting as you have seen it yourself.

From left to right: Eleazar de Carvalho (b. 1912), Olga Koussevitzky
(1901–78), Serge Koussevitzky (1874–1951) and Leonard Bernstein
(1918–90), at Tanglewood in 1949 (courtesy of The Berkshire Eagle,
Pittsfield, Mass.*)*

Good counsels, remarks and true orientation were failing him from such a great master as the illustrious Koussevitzky.

Heartily grateful for the kind consideration which you have granted me so many times, please transmit to the most distinguished niece of yours[8] the best greetings from myself and my wife.

Very affectionately, the friend ever faithful

Villa-Lobos

[8] The niece is Olga Koussevitzky (1901–78). Her aunt, Natalie (1882–1942), was Koussevitzky's first wife. After her death he married Olga, née Naumow, on 15 August 1947.

Manuscript first page of Madona (*courtesy of Éditions Max Eschig*)

In the following year Carvalho was even given an opportunity to conduct the Boston Symphony Orchestra, on 26 and 27 December 1947. Villa-Lobos had previously (LETTER 34, below) sounded out Koussevitzky to see if he could again guest-conduct the Orchestra. Koussevitzky decided, instead, to give the younger Brazilian conductor a chance to conduct his mentor's music; and so, among other works, Carvalho gave the North American premiere of Villa-Lobos' tone poem *Madona* (Villa-Lobos had conducted the world premiere in Rio de Janeiro, on 8 October 1946). The work was commissioned by The Serge Koussevitzky Music Foundation in the Library of Congress and is dedicated to the memory of Natalie Koussevitzky; it was composed in December 1945.

LETTER 34
VILLA-LOBOS TO SERGE KOUSSEVITZKY
Original: English

Rio, 27 de Junho de 1947

Mr. Dr. Serge Koussevitzky
Boston Symphony Orchestra
Boston, Massachusetts

Dear friend Dr. Koussevitzky:
As I intend come back in the United States next December to stay there till April, 1948, and if some arrangement can be made between now and then, I shall be delighted once more to be included in the schedule of guest conductors with your magnificent orchestra for next season, conducting one or two festivals of my works.

This would be also a great opportunity and an agreable occasion to see you personally again.

Any decision in such matter I ask you kindly send it to me (Rua Araujo Porto Alegre 56-5⁰-54-Rio de Janeiro – Brasil) or my manager (Henri Leiser – 164 West 79th Street New-York-24, N.Y.)

TEATRO MUNICIPAL

TEMPORADA OFICIAL DE CONCERTOS SINFONICOS·

com a ORQUESTRA MUNICIPAL

FESTIVAL VILLA-LOBOS

I.° CONCERTO

3 DE OUTUBRO DE 1946 - 21 hs.

PROGRAMA

I PARTE

I -- 1a. SINFONIA (Imprevisto) (1916)
    Allegro Moderato
    Adagio
    Scherzo
    Allegro con brio

II PARTE

II — MADONA — (Poêma Sinfonico) (1945)
                (1a. audição)
III — FANTASIA PARA CELO E ORQUESTRA
        (1945) (1a. audição)

Solista: IBERÊ GOMES GROSSO

III PARTE

IV — CAIXINHA DE BOAS FESTAS — (Poema
        Sinfonico e Bailado infantil) (1932)

Regencia: VILLA-LOBOS

Programme for the world premiere of Madona

In the hope of hearing from you soon, and antecipating the pleasure of working with your excellent orchestra next season, I remain,

Most cordially

Villa-Lobos

Adress: R. Araujo Porto Alegre 56-5º-54-Rio de Janeiro – Brasil

From 1944 onwards, as Villa-Lobos' thoughts turned more and more to the United States, his compositions tended to return to traditional forms. The Eighth String Quartet was composed in 1944, followed a year later by the Seventh Symphony. And it was in that year that the Canadian pianist Ellen Ballon (1898–1969) commissioned Villa-Lobos to write a composition for her. Again he chose a traditional form – the work is entitled simply 'Concerto No. 1 for Piano and Orchestra' – and dedicated the result to Ballon (it was to be followed between 1948 and 1957, by four more). Ellen Ballon had been a child prodigy, making her New York debut in 1910. She first toured Europe in 1927, and resided in England until the outbreak of World War II. She gave the world premiere of the First Piano Concerto, under the baton of the composer, in the Teatro Municipal in Rio de Janeiro on 11 October 1946, and the North American premiere, under Antal Doráti, in Dallas on 29 December of that year. The review in the *Dallas Morning News* the next day, by John Rosenfield, was not favourable. Doráti wrote of the premiere:[9]

I remember the premiere of the Villa-Lobos First Piano Concerto with Ellen Ballon very well – it was (is) a lovely romantic work, and was received very well.

[9] In a letter to me, dated 22 November 1983. Doráti (1906–88) will be remembered chiefly as a conductor, though he was active also as a composer. He studied with Kodály at the Liszt Academy in Budapest, where he made his debut as an operatic conductor at the age of 18. After conducting in Dresden and Münster, he moved to France and, in 1940, to the United States. Throughout his long career he held a series of prestigious posts, chronicled in his autobiography, *Notes from Eight Decades*, Hamish Hamilton, London, 1981.

Villa-Lobos' first recorded letter to Ellen Ballon refers to this performance.

LETTER 35

VILLA-LOBOS TO ELLEN BALLON

Original: English

Rio, 17 de Dezembro de 1946

Miss. E. Ballon

2 West 67th Street

New-York, 23, N.Y.

Dear Miss Ballon

In reply your amable letter of december 5th I want to thank you in my name and my wife, the gentilness of your words, that touched us deeply.

We were very sorry that you couldn't come to Buenos Aires, which is a great ciry to the artist and has a very good audience.

I hope other opportunity will come and I will not forget to include your name in a concert that I conduct.

Did you play my Piano's Concert with the Dallas Symphony Orchestra? We would like to know about the success that you have.

I and Mindinha[10] wish you a Happy Christmas and successful New-Year.

Sincerely yours

Villa-Lobos

Adress: R. Araujo Porto Alegre, 56-5º apart. 54 – Rio

On that same day Villa-Lobos wrote also to a friend of Ellen Ballon's, the Canadian poet and musician Ralph Gustafson (his father was Swedish and his mother Canadian), who was then making his living in New York as a free-lance writer; he returned to Canada in 1960.[11]

---

[10] His pet name for Arminda.

[11] Ralph Gustafson's reminiscences of Villa-Lobos appear as Appendix Two, on pp. 194–98; *cf.* also p. 99.

Villa-Lobos discussing aspects of his First Piano Concerto with Ellen Ballon (1898–1969) (courtesy of National Library of Canada, Ottawa)

LETTER 36
VILLA-LOBOS TO RALPH GUSTAFSON
Original: English

Rio, 17 de dezembro de 1946

Mr. Ralph Gustafson
2 West 66th Street
New-York, 23, N.Y.

My dear Mr. Gustafson
In reply your letter of the november 6th, I wish to thank you the good words and your book of the poetry, explendid work.
I have a great pleasure to say you that was to me of the much interest to know personalities as yours.

Manuscript first page of the First Piano Concerto
(courtesy of Éditions Max Eschig)

Antal Doráti
(1906–88),
photographed in
1985 (courtesy of
Martin Anderson)

I was very sorry that Miss Ballon couldn't come to Buenos Aires as were our wishes, but I think that some other opportunity will appear.

Remember us to all our friends. Happy Christmas and New-Year.

Sincerely yours,

Villa-Lobos

Adress: R. Araujo Porto Alegre, 56-6° apart. 54 – Rio

Four further letters testify to the mutual personal and professional admiration of Villa-Lobos and Ellen Ballon. He was naturally pleased that she performed his concerto in several other countries, including her native Canada. Arminda Villa-Lobos, who wrote much of the composer's correspondence in his name in those years (to which end she made a real effort to master French and English), refers to this event in the second letter to Ballon which is available – and which she also signed – from the following year.

```
        Rio, 17 de dezembro de 1946


Mr.Ralph Gustafson
2 West 66th Street
New-York,23,N.Y.



                .My dear Mr.Gustafson

        In reply your letter of the november 6th, I
   wish to thank you the good words and your book of
   the poetry, explendid work.
        I have a great pleasure to say you that was
   to me of the much interest to know personalities as
   yours.'
        I was very sorry that Miss Ballon couldn't
   come to Buenos Aires as were our wishes, but I think
   that some other opportunity will appear.
        Remember us to all friends. Happy Chrismas,
        Sincerely yours,                and New-Year


              Villa-Lobos

   Adress.R.Araujo Porto Alegre,56-5º apart.54-Rio
```

Letter (36) from Villa-Lobos to Ralph Gustafson
(courtesy of Ralph Gustafson)

LETTER 37
ARMINDA VILLA-LOBOS TO ELLEN BALLON
Original: English

Rio, May 28, 1947

My dear Miss Ballon
It was very nice to hear from you. I hope you and all friends are very happy and with very good health.
Happily I and my husband are very well. Meanwhile, you

must know that we have always many souvernirs of you.

I understood very well that you is kind with me about my *very, very, very bad English* (with music) but as I am not proud, I thank you very much.

I am satisfied if you understand what I wish to say. It is only that I want.

Next month, I must begin to learn English, and in that moment, I will write better. Perhaps my teacher can write to me . . .

Do you know the time of October that you will play your Concert in Montreal? If the concert is broadcast, I ask you to write me, because I will try to hear with Villa-Lobos.

When you will write to me in Portuguese? I am exciting to receive soon.

Our kindest regards to Mr. Gustafson.

Remembrances of Villa-Lobos.

Loves and 'saudades' of your friend

Arminda

R. Araujo Porto Alegre, 56-5º apart. -54 – Rio

LETTER 38
VILLA-LOBOS TO ELLEN BALLON
Original: English

Rio, 2 de junho de 1947

Miss Ellen Ballon
2 West 67th Street
New-York, 23, N.Y.
USA

Dear friend Miss Ballon

In reply your letter May 15, I ask you my excuses, I didn't write before, because I was very busy.

I and Mindinha remember always the hospitality that you had with us.

TEATRO MUNICIPAL

TEMPORADA OFICIAL DE CONCERTOS SINFONICOS

com a ORQUESTRA MUNICIPAL

2.º CONCERTO
II DE OUTUBRO DE 1946 - 21 hs.

PROGRAMA

I PARTE

I — BACHIANAS BRASILEIRAS N.º 7 (1942)
     ... Preludio (Ponteio)
     - Giga (Quadrilha caipira)
     -- Tocata (Desafio)
     .-- Fuga (Conversa)
II — 1.º CONCERTO DE PIANO E ORQUESTRA (1945)
       (Dedicado à Ellen Ballon) — (1.ª audição)
       — Allegro
       — Allegro — Poco Scherzando
       — Andante
       — Allegro non tropo
            Solista: ELLEN BALLON

II PARTE

III — DESCOBRIMENTO DO BRASIL (2.- Suite) 1937
            (1.ª auuição)
       — Impressão Moura
       — Adagio Sentimental
       — Cascavel
IV — MANDÚ-CÁRÁRÁ (Poema Sinfonico ou bailado ameríndio) (1940)

(Orquestra e córos) (Texto extraído de várias lendas amazonenses recolhidas por Barbosa Rodrigues) (1.ª audição)

COROS DO TEATRO MUNICIPAL E ORFEÃO DO EXTERNATO PEDRO II PREPARADOS PELO MAESTRO SANTIAGO GUERRA E PROFESSORAS MARIA PAULINA LOPES PATUREAU E ELZA COSTA LIMA

Regente: VILLA-LOBOS

Programme of the world premiere of the First Piano Concerto

We are very glad that you must come here in next year. If I had possibility to conduct with you, I will do with much pleasure.

In reference my work 'Caixinha de Boas Festas',[12] I think that Maestro Burle Marx[13] conducted in New-York once. I have no copy, but Associated[14] has. Please, ask Henri[15] that he can speak with Mrs Urban of the Associated to obtain this or other work, as 2ª *Suite do Descobrimento do Brasil*.[16]

Unhappily I have no more 'Danses Africaines' (Danses des Indiens Mestis[17]) printed in Max-Eschig (Rue de Rome 48-Paris). Associated Music Publishers is the representative of Max-Eschig.

Thank you your kindness to learn my music. I hope and Mindinha to hear them in somewhere.

I think this year I can[18] go to the United States, because it's impossible to Henri to promove some concerts to me.

[12] Villa-Lobos' *Caixinha de Boas Festas (Little Christmas Box)*, sometimes also known as *Vitrina Encantada (The Enchanted Shop-window)* is a symphonic poem, and is occasionally performed as a children's ballet.

[13] Walter Burle Marx (born 1902) is a Brazilian conductor; he trained as a pianist, first in Brazil, then in Germany, where he also took composition lessons. He has lived in Philadelphia since 1952. His own compositions include several orchestral pieces; he has also written on Brazilian music. He conducted a part of *Caixinha de Boas Festas* in one of his children's concerts in Rio on 23 November 1932 and the entire work on 8 December that year in the Teatro Municipal there.

[14] Associated Music Publishers, Inc., the American representatives of Éditions Max Eschig, Villa-Lobos' Paris publishers.

[15] *Cf.* note 7 on p. 81.

[16] *Cf.* note 3 on p. 76.

[17] That is, the *Danças Características Africanas; cf.* also p. 24. 'Mestis' means 'half-cast'.

[18] The sense indicates that a negative is missing.

How is Mr. Gustafson? I like his information about Marks Co.,[19] the true thieves of my musics.

My warmest personal regards to you and Mr. Gustafson of Mindinha and

Villa-Lobos

Adress: R. Araujo Porto Alegre, 56-5º apart. 54 Rio de Janeiro-Brasil

LETTER 39

**HEITOR AND ARMINDA VILLA-LOBOS
TO ELLEN BALLON**

Original: English

Very bad English

Hotel Roblin
6, Rue Chauveau-Lagarde
Paris, (8ᵉ)

Paris, July, 26, 1947

My dear friend Miss Ballon

It was a very great pleasure to hear from you.

We have in Paris until 31, day that we go to the Rome, when I shall conduct at 6 in Augustes. After we go to the Lisbon and my concert is 14. Of the Lisbon, we come back to Paris and I will conduct 21 in the Theatre of Champ Elysees. Perhaps we go to London, but we dont know yet the date. It was very good of you was with us playing yours concert piano, but we hope sooner it was possible.

I think it was a good idea and you were very kind to

---

¹⁹ Villa-Lobos is presumably referring to Edward B. Marks Music Corporation, who had included his *A Prole do Bebê*, No. 1, as Album No. 16 in their series 'Contemporary Masterpieces'. It was also published by Arthur Napoleão, Éditions Max Eschig and Consolidated Music Publishers.

remember of my works to Mr. Weisemann[20] and Defauw[21] to play them. Descobrimento do Brasil (1st Suite) is a duration 13 minutes, but Bachianas n. 4 about 25 minutes.

We liked very much the choice that you did of my piano soli. Thank you for all.

We hope we can hear the Piano Concert in October 28th next.

It was very nice to see the picture in the Musical Courier of New-York, and we hope to receive a copy of the Montreal Standard too.

In the hoping to see you and your good friend Mr. Gustafson veri soon, we send you our 'saudades'.

Most cordially, yours friends

Arminda & Villa-Lobos

(I hope you can understand what I wrote in English and without 'typewriter'. I did many efforts to write with a *calligraphie* that you can read.

Loves

Arminda

(L'adress: Ambassade du Brésil
          Av. Montaigne, 45
          Paris – France

[20] According to Ralph Gustafson (letter to me, dated 28 January 1984), this 'must be Frieder Weissmann. He was conductor in Europe. He recorded the famous set of records of Rosenthal playing the E-minor piano concerto of Chopin (Parlophon 9558 etc.), he went to Argentina and there married Rosita (did not know her maiden name) and came to New York where I knew them both. He became conductor of the New Jersey Symphony'.

[21] The Belgian conductor Désiré Defauw (1885–1960) was also a noted violinist, and for a period (1914–18) led his own quartet (its violist was Lionel Tertis). He held conducting appointments in Brussels and New York, and from 1943 to 1947 was conductor of the Chicago Symphony Orchestra.

LETTER 40
VILLA-LOBOS TO ELLEN BALLON
Original: English

Rio, 9 de Setembro de 1947

My dear Miss Ballon:

It was a great pleasure to hear from you. We remember always our good friend.

When I organized my concerts in Europe, I included your name in the programs. I hope you could play in Paris with me conducting Orchestra Pasdeloup Fevrier 29th, Rome with Orchestra de la Accademia de Santa Cecilia, etc. As the situation of the Europe is very difficult, I can not give you the confirmation because the 'cachet', but when I have some news I will write you immediately.

Many thanks for all kindness. You always nice with good words, actions, etc.

We like very much the photograph of the three of us and a copy the Saturday Review of Literature.

I thank Mr. Gustafson to write an editorial and I hope to receive a copy.

I wrote to Leiser about my festival in Colombia. I will have much pleasure to conduct you again.

When I was in Paris, Mtro Victor Brault,[22] director de 'La Cantoria (4046 Rue Tupper-Montreal) invited me to conduct my own works in Montreal and Toronto, in December, and I gave him your name to play your Concert. Do you like it? I asked him to write to Henri and you.

---

[22] Victor Brault (1899–1963), a native Canadian, began his career as a distinguished baritone, studying in Paris: in recitals there in 1922 and 1923, for example, he performed songs by Fauré, Honegger, Roussel and Tansman, accompanied in each case by the composer; Ravel, too, directed Brault's performance in London, in 1923, of his *Trois Poèmes de Mallarmé*. Brault founded La Cantoria, a Montreal choir with a nucleus of approximately 30 voices, around 1939 (although he was not its exclusive conductor); its early years included performances of music by Lili Boulanger, Honegger, Pierné and Tansman, as well as works by Canadian composers. The choir disbanded in the early 1950s.

Ralph Gustafson (b. 1909) photographed during a visit to Sally Ryan's High Perch Farm in Connecticut, in 1955 – cf. note 26 on p. 105 (courtesy of Ralph Gustafson)

We are happy to meet you in Rio next season, because I will come back beginning June, when you must go.

Mindinha is very sorry with her English. She says that she speaks very bad, *now*. It's true *now* or *always?*

We hope to see you and Mr. Gustafson very soon.

With our souvenirs, yours sincerely

Villa-Lobos

R. Araujo Porto Alegre 56-5°-54
Rio de Janeiro – Brasil

The first Canadian performance took place on 28 October 1947 in the Auditorium du Plateau at Montreal, under Désiré Defauw; it was presented by the International Service of the Canadian

Désiré Defauw
_(1885–1960)_
(courtesy of the
Société
Philharmonique de
Bruxelles)

Broadcasting Corporation before an invited audience and was also broadcast to South America by shortwave radio. 'The program was presented free of charge to any Canadian who wanted to hear it. And many did. Three quarters of an hour before the concert began, they were lined up outside the hall, standing there in spite of the thinly spattering rain', as Thomas Archer reported in _The Gazette_ of Montreal the day after the concert, in an extensive review of the event. 'It was the first concert in Canada entirely given over to works of Villa-Lobos and not just the performance of the concerto' – the programme also included the Third Suite from _Descobrimento do Brasil_.

Villa-Lobos' next letter to Ralph Gustafson dates from a year after his first. In it he refers to the Montreal performance of the first Piano Concerto and to the forthcoming premiere, on 23 January 1948 in New York, of his 'cantata profana', _Mandú-Çárárá_,[23]

[23] According to an indigenous legend collected by João Barbosa Rodrigues (1842–1909), a well-known Brazilian botanist, anthropologist and ethnologist, Mandú-Cárárá was a mysterious and pretty young Indian boy who was considered the incarnation of the dance. The title of Villa-Lobos' cantata is sometimes given as _Mandu-Çarará_.

by the Schola Cantorum of New York, under the direction of Hugh Ross (1898–1990), an old friend of Villa-Lobos from his days in Paris. The cantata was given not in its full orchestral version but in a version for two pianos, percussion, mixed chorus and children's chorus; the piano parts were played by Pierre Luboshutz (1894-1971) and Genia Nemenoff (1903–89).

LETTER 41
VILLA-LOBOS TO RALPH GUSTAFSON
Original: English

Rio, 1/12/1947

Mr. Ralph Gustafson
2, West Sixty Seventh Street
New-York 23, N.Y.

Dear friend:

Answering your letter of November, 25th, I am very glad to thank you for your kindness, and your very good article in the 'World'.[24]

I have heard from several friends that the concert was a great success for Miss Ballon. I was hoping for this.

If it's possible to have some records, I shall be pleased to obtain them.

I am going to try to hear my 'Mandú-Çárárá' on January 23rd, but if it's impossible I will try to obtain a record.

Hoping to see you and Miss Ballon, very soon, I remain always,

Cordially yours,
H. Villa-Lobos

R. Araujo Porto Alegre 56-5°-54
Rio de Janeiro
Brasil

---

[24] 'Carioca Commentary', *United Nations World*, Vol. 1, No. 10, December 1947, pp. 27–29 (letter to me from Ralph Gustafson, dated 10 February 1989); the citizens of Rio de Janeiro are known as 'Cariocas', after a brook, the Carioca, which runs through Rio.

From the spring of the following year there survives a short note in which Villa-Lobos gives Ralph Gustafson a sort of 'musical power of attorney' to conduct the First Piano Concerto, reproduced in facsimile opposite. But Gustafson is an amateur musician only and he was never to have the opportunity to do so.

LETTER 42
VILLA-LOBOS TO WHOM IT MAY CONCERN
Original: French

Villa-Lobos Music Corporation
1650 Broadway, New York 19, N.Y.

– An authorisation from a musician to a poet

I authorise my friend, poet and musician of heart, Ralph Gustafson, to conduct in my place, the 1st Piano Concerto which I have dedicated to our friend Ellen Ballon

To the moon, $\dfrac{5}{14}$

$\overline{48}$

Villa-Lobos

I have not been able to establish whether the Montreal and Toronto concerts mentioned in LETTER 40 took place or not. What is certain is that Ellen Ballon played the First Piano Concerto again, on 30 and 31 January 1951, with the Montreal Symphony Orchestra under Ernest Ansermet (1883–1969).

In the last letter to have been preserved from this exchange, Villa-Lobos refers to Ellen Ballon's recording, for Decca, of the First Piano Concerto, made in 1949, with Ernest Ansermet conducting the Orchestre de la Suisse Romande; Gustafson provided the sleeve notes.

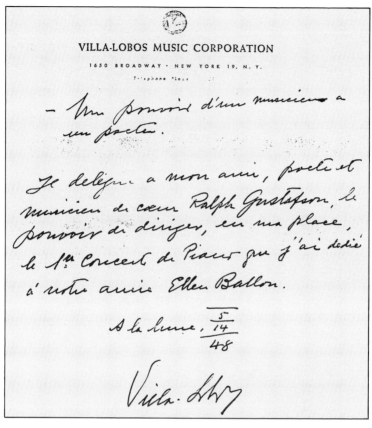

Villa-Lobos' 'musical power of attorney' for Ralph Gustafson
(cf. LETTER 42; courtesy of Ralph Gustafson)

LETTER 43
VILLA-LOBOS TO RALPH GUSTAFSON
Original: English

Rio, January 1950

Mr. Ralph Gustafson
2 West 67th Street
New-York 23 N.Y.
Dear friend:
Only today I am going to reply your nice letter of 6th
December, because I could not do before.

*The set of games
given to Villa-Lobos
by Ellen Ballon
(courtesy of the
Museu Villa-Lobos)*

I was very happy with the good news about the records of our friend Ellen, but I am very sorry, because until now I did not receive any record. I can not understand why Decca did not send for me.

The cable that you send, gave me very much pleasure. Many Thanks for all.

I want to see the album with the very good article of you. Our congratulations for this victory.

Unfortunately we can not meet the Trio-friends,[25] but I hope the next year it is possible.

Happy 1950.

With our best souvenirs,

Cordially,
Villa-Lobos

The relationship of Villa-Lobos and Arminda with Ellen Ballon was obviously very cordial, as is revealed in the letters and in the gift of a set of various table games from the pianist to the composer (it is now in the Museu Villa-Lobos in Rio de Janeiro). Nonetheless,

[25] Presumably Villa-Lobos, Arminda and Gustafson.

the correspondence seems to have come to a close five years after Villa-Lobos' last recorded letter to her in a Christmas telegram:

MERRY CHRISTMAS HAPPY NEW YEAR TAMMIE[26] ELLEN RALPH AMITIES

ARMINDA VILLA-LOBOS

In the summer of 1948 Villa-Lobos went into hospital in New York to undergo surgery for cancer of the bladder. It must have been immediately before or after his operation that, nothing daunted, and obviously expecting a full recovery, he wrote to the British Council to try to arrange some concerts in London. On 16 July 1948 parts of this letter (the original has not been located) were then communicated by the British Council to the BBC; hence its fragementary nature. Seymour Whinyates was Director of Music at the British Council from 1943 until 1960.

LETTER 44
VILLA-LOBOS TO SEYMOUR WHINYATES
Original: French

[...] As you may recall, you kindly communicated me that you would centralise my concert activities in London in case of my return to this great city in 1949 considering that I would only return to London if there is an opportunity to conduct at least five concerts to compensate my expenses and to justify officially my absence from my country. You can also take it up with my friend Hate.[27]

I have only 15 days between 15 and 30 March (1949) to stay in England [...].

---

[26] According to a letter to me from Ralph Gustafson, dated 8 February 1989, 'Tammy' (in his spelling) was Sally Ryan, 'an American sculptress whose home in Georgetown, Connecticut, I used to visit and who was a close friend of Ellen Ballon [...]. It was farmland overlooking Long Island Sound and Villa-Lobos and Arminda enjoyed week-ends there when they came to New York'.

[27] 'Hate' has not been identified.

[...] The other dates you can arrange with my friend Hate, 2 programmes for 2 concerts with the BBC, and with other orchestras which you deem possible, also with Barbirolli's one [...].

B.B.C. *(First Programme)*

Bachianas Brasileiras (No. 3) Piano and Orch.		30 minutes
First Symphony		20 minutes
Choros No. 12	Full Orchestra	40 minutes

B.B.C. *(Second Programme)*

Second Symphony		50 minutes
Rudepoêma	Full Orchestra	30 minutes

[...] All the orchestral material is with Maison Max-Eschig-Rue de Rome, 48-Paris [...].

The English musicologist Edward Lockspeiser (1905–73) is best remembered for his writings on French music, particularly his work on Debussy.[28] At the time of Villa-Lobos' letter to him, Lockspeiser was Overseas Information and Research Assistant for the Music Department of the BBC.[29] A note pencilled on the letter reads 'Await reply', followed by the signature of Peter Crossley-Holland, who at the time was Music Assistant in the Music Department, and the date, 14/XII.[30] Crossley-Holland's reply followed just under a month later.

[28] Lockspeiser studied in Paris with Nadia Boulanger and Alexandre Tansman. His writings also include studies of Berlioz and Bizet.

[29] The BBC Music Department at this time produced programmes both for domestic broadcasting and for the Overseas Service; Villa-Lobos' invitation was for a broadcast on the (domestic) Third Programme.

[30] Peter Crossley-Holland (b. 1916) is also a musicologist of some distinction. A pupil of John Ireland, Mátyás Seiber and Julius Harrison, he also studied Indian music at the School of African and Oriental Studies in London. He had been at the Arts Council for two years (1943–45) before joining the BBC in 1948, leaving in 1963 to take up academic posts in Berlin and then California. In 1965 he became editor of the *Journal of the International Folk Music Council*. He retired in 1984. His writings are chiefly on Celtic, Tibetan and native American music, and his compositions include works for chorus, solo voices and recorders.

LETTER 45
VILLA-LOBOS TO EDWARD LOCKSPEISER
Original: French

Rio, 28 November 1948

Mr. Edward Lockspeiser

Sir:

In answer to your kind letter of 18 November, I inform you that it is impossible for me to go to London at the beginning of March because I must conduct some concerts in Paris and on 6 March is already the first concert.

As I had the pleasure to tell Miss Seymur,[31] my dear friend, I could dispose time to conduct in England, which I admire so much, between 15 and 30 March. Believe me it will be a great honour to conduct concerts within the programme where you see a possibility.

Concerning the concert of the Radiodiffusion Française, I agree that some steps should be taken for its broadcast to London but herein I have no say because this is a matter for Radio française.

I look forward to hearing from you as soon as possible because at the beginning of next January I must go to North America to realise some festivals of my works in that country and afterwards to Mexico, Paris, Rome, Barcelona, Madrid, etc. I thank you for your interest in my participation in your great country, and send you my regards.

Very cordially

Villa-Lobos

R. Araújo Porto Alegre 56
Rio de Janeiro
Brazil

---

[31] Presumably Miss Seymour Whinyates at the British Council.

*Villa-Lobos with Arminda and Ralph Gustafson at High Perch Farm,
on 24 September 1948 (courtesy of Ralph Gustafson)*

LETTER 46
PETER CROSSLEY-HOLLAND TO VILLA-LOBOS
Original: English

35, Marylebone High Street, W. 1 (WELbeck 5577)
Reference 03071/M/PCH

10th January, 1949

Dear Mr. Villa-Lobos,

Mr. Lockspeiser has passed on to me your letter of 28th November, 1948. We are delighted to hear that you might possibly arrange to visit England sometime during the period 15th-30th March. We should indeed be very pleased if you would be willing to conduct the BBC Symphony Orchestra on 26th March in the Third Programme. Sir Adrian Boult will be conducting part of this concert and we much hope that you will be able to suggest a work of your own which you would like to conduct. From our point of view it would be interesting if you could do a work not yet heard in this country.

I should mention that we are giving two concerts of Latin-American music on 5th and 17th March under Clarence Raybould and Anthony Bernard respectively. In the first of these we are hoping to include your Choros No. 10 and in the second your Choros Nos. 3 and 7. No. 10 has not been heard before in this country and it would be pleasant for us if, on 26th March, you would be able to give us a further work.

I much look forward to hearing from you as soon as possible so that we may go ahead with the arrangements for this concert. When we hear what work you suggest perhaps you could let me know the duration of it, the exact instrumentation and where the orchestral material can be obtained, and also how many rehearsals would be desirable.

Yours very sincerely
Peter Crossley-Holland

Mr. H. Villa-Lobos
R. Araujo,
Porto Alegre 56,
Rio de Janeiro,
Brazil

*A photograph of Villa-Lobos and Arminda in 1948, inscribed to Ralph
Gustafson, taken two months before the composer entered the Memorial
Hospital in New York for an operation for cancer of the bladder; the
caption reads 'Attention! This is not Churchill! This is Villa-Lobos and
his wife talking with his friend Ralph Gustafson, but not about the
war . . . it is about his great talent as poet and artist'
(courtesy of Ralph Gustafson)*

Villa-Lobos' Seventh Symphony had been composed for a competi-
tion in Detroit and entered under the pseudonym of 'A.
Caramuru'.[32]

> On the initiative of Harry Relchold,[33] president of the Detroit
> Symphony Orchestra, a grand competition will be held to
> select the 'Symphony of the Americas' for which composers
> of the Continent can apply. It was established that these
> works, a symphony or a symphonic poem, should have a
> length of 25 to 35 minutes and must be submitted by 1 July.
> On 1 September the first three winners will be announced.

[32] *Cf.* the Villa-Lobos catalogue, *Villa-Lobos – Sua Obra*, published by the
Museu Villa-Lobos, Rio de Janeiro, 2nd edn., 1972, p. 171, and 3rd edn.,
1989, p. 64.

[33] The correct name is Henry H. Reichhold; he was a multi-millionaire
chemical magnate who also owned the Music Hall in Detroit (letter from
Charles Pantely, Public Relations Department of the Detroit Symphony
Orchestra, dated 10 August 1989).

The first prize will be approximately 500,000 cruzeiros, the second prize 100,000 cruzeiros and the third prize 50,000 cruzeiros.[34]

According to the Museu Villa-Lobos in Rio de Janeiro,[35] Villa-Lobos's symphony won first prize. But this is not so. The winner of the $25,000 first prize of the Reichhold award was Professor Leroy Robertson, head of the music department at Brigham Young University at Provo, Utah, for his composition *Trilogy*; there was also a second prize of $5,000 and a third prize of $2,500. Villa-Lobos was not even mentioned, according to *The Detroit Free Press* for 10 December 1945, which also states that 'the Detroit Symphony Orchestra will present the three prize-winning symphonies at successive concerts next fall'.[36] Since Villa-Lobos' Symphony had yet to be performed, it seemed an ideal response to Crossley-Holland's request. The world premiere duly took place on 26 March 1949, performed by the BBC Symphony Orchestra[37] under the baton of the composer, and broadcast on the Third Programme of the BBC.

LETTER 47
VILLA-LOBOS TO PETER CROSSLEY-HOLLAND
Original: French

Paris, 11 February, 1949

Hotel Roblin
6 Rue Chauveau Lagarde
Paris 8ᵉ

Mr. Peter Crossley-Holland
35, Marylebone High Street, W.1.

Dear Sir:

I have pleasure of sending you the title of the music which I am to conduct on 26 March.

It is my Seventh Symphony, which will be a world premiere with the BBC.

[34] *Correio Paulista*, São Paulo, 8 April 1945.

[35] Letter to me from Helena A. Araujo Góes of the Museu Villa-Lobos, dated 22 March 1989.

[36] Letter from Charles Pantely, dated 10 August 1989.

[37] Not the London Symphony Orchestra and not 27 March, as claimed in *Villa-Lobos – Sua Obra*, 2nd edn., 1972, p. 171, and 3rd edn., 1989, p. 64, and in David P. Appleby, *Heitor Villa-Lobos: A Bio-Bibliography*, Greenwood Press, Westport and London 1988, p. 103.

```
21.11      MUSIC OF LATIN AMERICA
           (Music Dept.)
                        The BBC Chorus
                  (Chorus-Master : Leslie Woodgate)
                     BBC Symphony Orchestra
                       (Leader: Paul Beard)
                     Extras :            J.Lees (Jnr.)(percussion)
                                         C.S.Norrington (percussion)
                                         L. Brain (Bass Oboe)
                                         R.Parker (tenor trombone)
                                         H.J.Curran (4th cornet
                                           . and trumpet)
                                         W. Davey (piano and Celesta)
                                         I. Berry (Celesta)
                                         A.Dulay (Celesta) (One
                                                    rehearsal only)
                        Conducted by : Clarence Raybould


22.14      MUSIC OF LATIN AMERICA  -  PART 2
           Cuauhnahuac        (11'00")      Silvestre      Schirmer
              (First performance             Revueltas
               in England)                   (Mexico)
           Tonada No.11       (5'00")       Humberto.      Senart
              (First performance             Allende
               in England)                   (Chile)
           Choros No.10       (15'00")      Heitor         Eschig
              (First performance             Villa Lobos
               in England)                   (Brazil)


22.46½     PROGRAMME TRAILER AND RECORD FILL-UP
              Ondine (Debussy)                         COL.LB.61
              Casadesus                                2'27"


22.50      CHRISTMAS REMEMBERED
           (Talks Dept.)
                        (Repeat of the recording broadcast in the Third
                         Programme on 25.12.1948 : SLO 43398)


23.10½     RECITAL
           (Music Dept.)              See att
                        The Consort of Viols of the Schola
                        Cantorum Basiliensis
                            August Wenzinger (treble viol and
                               viola da gamba)
                            Marianne Majer (tenor viol)
                            Maya Wenzinger (tenor viol)
                            Gertrud Flugel (bass viol)
                        John Wills (harpsichord)
           Tanzsatze for four viols        Johann         Schott
                        (8'00")            Staden
```

The two BBC programmes of 1949 (courtesy

```
21.40   MUSIC FROM LATIN AMERICA
              (Music Dept.)
                                          with
                              The London Chamber Singers
                              The London Chamber Orchestra
                                 Leader: Andrew Cooper
                                 Conductor: Anthony Bernard
                              Frederick Fuller  (Baritone)


        MUSIC FROM LATIN AMERICA (contd.)
           Canzone for Strings
              Nunqua fue pena Maior
                 (First performance in England)
                              4'00"
                                          Juan Urrade
                                          (15th Century Spanish)
                                                          MS
                 Three Native Songs             Traditional
                                                (Peru)     Libraire Orientale
                 Inca Hymn to the Sun
                 As, Sumak Kabcakchaska   (Male Voices)
                              1'45"
                 Political Song
                    Pikota Kasata (Mixed Voices)
                              1'00"
                 Love Song
                    Tristezas me Depara (Solo Voice)
                              4'15"
                       (First performance in England)
           Chorus No. 7 for seven instruments
                              9'00"
                                          Villa-Lobos
                                          (Brazil)    Chester
           Lamentations of Jeremiah for
              unaccompanied chorus
                              12'00"
                                          Alberto Ginastera
                                          (Argentine) Music Press Inc.
                       (First performance in England)
           Colorines for Orchestra
                              7'00"
                                          Silvestre Revueltas
                                          (Mexico)   MS
                       (First performance in England)
           Pica-Pau (Chorus No. 5) for
              Male voice Chorus and Seven
              Wind Instruments
                              4'00"
                                          Heitor Villa-
                                          Lobos        Eschig


22.55   FROM OUR OWN CORRESPONDENT
                       Read by Christopher Serpell
              (Pre-recorded 16.5.1949 - DLO 49366)
```

of BBC Written Archives, Caversham)

I have suggested this music to you because you wrote me that in London they are about to play my Choros 3, 7 and 10, and I myself have already conducted in London Choros 6.

I think this Symphony will be more varied and more interesting because it is one of my recent works and because it is a type completely different from all the others.

I first thought of 'Choros No. 9' is the work but it has almost the same number of instruments and length too.

I think the 7th Symphony can be presented.

Enclosed please find the nomenclature of the two works and their duration.

I need four rehearsals.

Please send me your definite reply about the music, and I also request you to obtain for me the document which I need to enter London to conduct, because last time I had some difficulties with the Immigration concerning this paper.

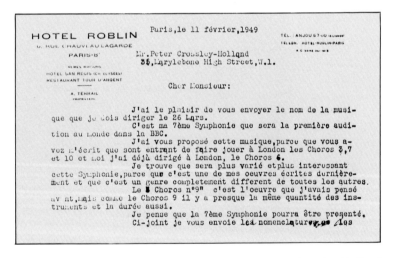

Letter (47) from Villa-Lobos to Peter Crossley-Holland

I await your letter in order to send you at once the programme notes of the work that will be presented.

With my most cordial greetings

H. Villa-Lobos

Adress: Hotel Roblin: – 6 Rue Chauveau Lagarde
Paris-France

It was in 1949 that Villa-Lobos' correspondence with Irving Schwerké seems to have resumed, after a gap that may well remain unexplained. It was in that year that Villa-Lobos was one of eleven composers commissioned by UNESCO in Paris to write a work for a gala concert, in the Salle Gaveau on 3 October 1949, commemorating the centenary of Chopin's death.

deux musiques avec la durée.
Je besoin de quatre repetitions.
S'il vous plaît, envoyez moi la réponse definitif sur la
musique et je vous demande aussi, obtenir le document que je dois en -
trer à London pour diriger,parce que l'autre fois,j'ai eu quelque dif
ficulté à l'imigration à cause de ce papier.
J'attenderais la votre lettre pour envoyer toute suit le
commentaire de l'oeuvre que sera presenté.

Avec mes salutations très cordiales,

H.Villa-Lobos

Adress: Hotel Roblin: – 6,rue Chauveau Lagarde
Paris-France

(courtesy of BBC Written Archives, Caversham)

LETTER 48
VILLA-LOBOS TO IRVING SCHWERKÉ
Original: French

Ministry of Education and Health

Rio, 12 August, 1949

Mr. Irving Scherke
320 East Wisconsin Avenue
Appleton, Wisconsin
USA

Dear Friend:

It was for me a great pleasure to receive your letter of 10 July.

I reply only today because I was in S. Paulo where I have some symphony concerts with my works.

I am very glad to know that you have a good artistic position, and I hope to hear you one day.

You did very well to remind me of the dedication I promised you and you can be sure that next time I shall do some piano music for you.

Although I don't know English, I watch nevertheless the programme, etc., and some of your articles about me. Thank you very much.

It is regrettable that we cannot meet in North America where I have gone almost every year, since 1944.

Last year, at this time, I was in the United States, not to give concerts but because of my health. I was in the hospital in New York for two months where I passed some terrible days after some very dangerous surgery. Fortunately, Dr. Marshall gave me back my life[38] and I continue since December to give concerts as usual.

Since 1947 I have returned to Europe where I have always given concerts. Next year I am to go to many countries in Europe. For North America, I have not yet received anything positive from my manager in New York, but if something is being organised there, I should be there from the end

---

[38] Dr Victor Marshall was Villa-Lobos' surgeon.

P R O G R A M M E

ALLOCUTION par M. ROLAND-MANUEL
Président de la Commission préparatoire
du Conseil international de la musique

Tombeau de Chopin (pour quintette à cordes) .... ALEXANDRE TANSMAN
1. Nocturne
2. Mazurka
3. Postlude
le QUATUOR CALVET
et GASTON LOGEROT (contrebasse)

Hommage à Chopin (pour piano) .... HEITOR VILLA-LOBOS
1. Nocturne
2. A la Ballade

Sonate espagnole (pour piano) .... OSCAR ESPLA
1. Andante romantico
2. Mazurka sopra un tema popolare
3. Allegro brioso
ARNALDO ESTRELLA

Étude-Caprice (pour violoncelle) .... JACQUES IBERT
MAURICE MARÉCHAL

Suite polonaise (pour soprano et piano) .... ANDRZEJ PANUFNIK
1. Praeludium
2. Allegretto
3. Interludium
4. Vivo
5. Postludium
IRENE JOACHIM et ANDRÉ COLLARD

Pastorale (pour hautbois et piano) .... HOWARD HANSON
JULES GOETGHELUCK et l'AUTEUR

Trois Mazurkas (pour piano) .... LENNOX BERKELEY
1. Allegro
2. Allegretto
3. Allegro

Hommage à Chopin ; (pour piano) .... G. F. MALIPIERO
Étude .... CARLOS CHAVEZ
HÉLÈNE PIGNARI

Mazurka-Nocturne (pour hautbois, 2 violons et violoncelle) .... BOHUSLAV MARTINU
JULES GOETGHELUCK, GEORGES TESSIER,
GEORGES HUGON et ROGER ALBIN

Ode à Frédéric Chopin .... FLORENT SCHMITT
Sur un texte poétique de Frédéric Nietzsche
(pour chœur à 4 voix mixtes et piano)
l'ENSEMBLE VOCAL MARCEL COURAUD
et ANDRÉ COLLARD

Concert programme of the UNESCO Gala Concert (courtesy of UNESCO)

The first pages of the two parts of Hommage à Chopin

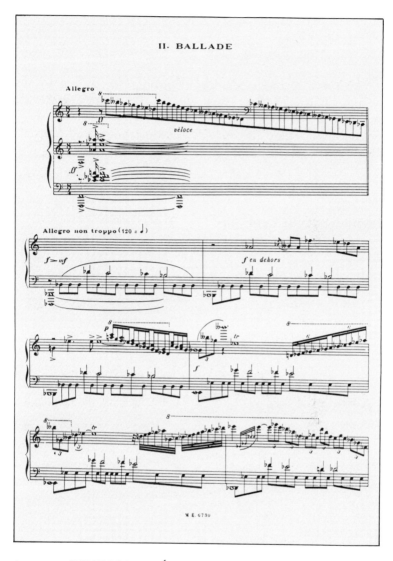

(courtesy of UNESCO and Éditions Max Eschig)

of December until February. Let's see if it will be possible to be together then.

I sent you yesterday some piano music which you don't know.

Have you already seen the recordings which I did with C.B.S.? Bachianas Brasileiras No. 5 – Bidú Sayão and celli, was considered the best record in 1946.

Looking forward to your news, I am sending you my very affectionate greetings.

Cordially

Villa-Lobos

R. Araujo Porto Alegre 56
Rio de Janeiro
Brazil

[Added in handwriting]
I have dedicated to you 'Hommage à Chopin' of which I have sent you a copy.

LETTER 49
VILLA-LOBOS TO IRVING SCHWERKÉ
Original: French

Rio, 10 November, 1949

Mr. Irving Schwerké
320 East Wisconsin Ave.
Appleton, Wisconsin
USA

Dear Friend:
Only today have I had the opportunity of replying to your very kind letter because I was very busy with concerts in my country and with the Department which I run in Rio.

Until now I am not sure if I go to the United States but if I have concerts, I shall be very happy to write to you to see if it is possible to meet again.

I am waiting for 'Hommage à Chopin' to be printed to send you a copy. If you want to have a manuscript copy with the dedication, tell me so and I shall send it to you at once.

Thank you for the kind words you sent me.

With every cordial remembrances

Villa-Lobos

R. Araujo Porto Alegre 56
Rio de Janeiro
Brazil

LETTER 50
VILLA-LOBOS TO IRVING SCHWERKÉ
Original: French

Rio, 11 December 1949

Mr. Irving Scherké
320 East Wisconsin Ave.
Appleton, Wisconsin
USA

Dear Friend:

In reply to your letter of 27 November, I inform you that I have sent the music manuscript with the dedication, and I believe we will have the music in print in a few months.

This year I shall not go to the United States. I shall be at home until February and thereafter I shall leave for Europe where I have concerts.

I sent you my sincere wishes for a Merry Christmas and 1950.

Very affectionate rememberances from

Villa-Lobos

Rua Araujo Porto Alegre 56
Rio de Janeiro
Brazil

LETTER 51
VILLA-LOBOS TO IRVING SCHWERKÉ
Original: French

Ministry of Education and Health

Rio, June 1950

Mr. Irving Schwerké
320 East Wisconsin Ave.
Appleton, Wisconsin
USA

Dear Friend:

As I was on an artistic tour in the states of Brazil and returned a few days ago, I am replying only today to your kind letter of 22 February.

Unfortunately, until today your 'Hommage à Chopin' is not yet printed, and to give you pleasure I send you a heliograph copy with my dedication, as you requested.[39]

I don't have your book 'Views and Interviews'[40] and I shall be delighted to receive a copy.

With every affectionate remembrances,

Villa-Lobos

R. Araujo Porto Alegre 56
Rio de Janeiro
Brazil

[39] As LETTERS 48, 49 and 51 reveal, Villa-Lobos must have sent Irving Schwerké a (presumably heliograph) copy; Schwerké then seems to have requested another copy, with an inscription.

[40] 4th edn., privately printed for the author by Les Orphelins-apprentis d'Auteuil, Paris, 1936.

VILLA-LOBOS TO IRVING SCHWERKÉ
Original: French

Brazilian Academy of Music

Rio, October, 8, 1950

Mr. Irving Schwerke
320 East Wisconsin Avenue
Appleton, Wisconsin

My dear Friend:

Only today I am replying to your kind letter of 29 July because I was in the United States where I had surgery, once again, at the memorial Hospital in New York where I was for two months.

Fortunately, I am feeling very well now and completely recovered from my illness. The surgery went magnificently and I hope I shall have no more bad days like those I have just had.

'Hommage à Chopin' is not yet printed but you can be sure that after it is in print I shall send you some copies.

Thank you for your book 'Views and Interviews'. Unfortunately, I shall not be able to read [it] as I don't know English but my wife can read some of it and will try to translate it for me.

Looking forward to your news, I am sending you my affectionate remembrance.

Villa-Lobos

Rua Araujo Porto Alegre 56
Rio de Janeiro
Brazil

LETTER 53
VILLA-LOBOS TO IRVING SCHWERKÉ
Original: French

Rio, January, 1951

Ministry of Education and Health

Mr. Irving Schwerke
New-York

Dear Friend:

It is a great pleasure for me to thank you for your good wishes which you sent me, and I shall be very glad if you would also have a 1951 full of good things as you deserve, and that we shall meet to talk face to face about the days when we had such a pleasant opportunity to be together in Paris.

Fortunately, I am completely recovered and I should continue my tour in Europe where I have concerts in several countries.

Looking forward to your news and in the hope of seeing you again soon, I am your devoted friend.

Villa-Lobos

Rua Araujo Porto Alegre 56
Rio de Janeiro
Brazil

LETTER 54
VILLA-LOBOS TO IRVING SCHWERKÉ
Original: French

Rio de Janeiro, 13 August, 1952

H. Villa-Lobos
R. Araujo Porto Alegre 56 – Apt. 54
Rio de Janeiro
Brazil

Mr. Irving Schwerke
USA

Dear Friend

Only today do I have the pleasure to thank you for your kind Christmas wishes as well as the good news that you have received the Légion d'Honneur because I was on an artistic tour in the United States and Europe and returned a few days ago.

My congratulations on this honour. I also had the great joy in 1948 having been elected by the Institute of France, and in 1949, in the presence of my friends Koussevitzky and Florent Schmitt, I received at the French Embassy in Rio, the *Croix d'Officier* of the Légion d'Honneur, which made me very happy.

I shall arrive in New York in December and I hope to have the chance to meet you at the Hotel NEW WESTON.

Thanking you for your kindness, I wish you all the best,

Affectionately

Villa-Lobos

LETTER 55
VILLA-LOBOS TO IRVING SCHWERKÉ
Original: French

Hotel New Weston
Madison Ave. at Fiftieth St.
New York 22, N.Y.

New-York, 1 March 1953

Mr. Irving Schwerke
320 East Wisconsin Avenue
Appleton Wisconsin

My dear Friend,

Only today arrived your letter of 25 December, sent to
Rio, and I am pleased to thank you for your interest in *your*
'HOMAGE À CHOPIN', by coincidence I have a copy here
in New-York which I am sending you as you requested.[41] It
is not yet printed but I hope that very soon, you shall have
the surprise to have it already published.

Since 9 December I have been on tour in the United States
and Venezuela, and this evening I shall leave for Europe
where I have concerts in Paris, London, Barcelona, Vienna,
Athens, Scala of Milan, etc. and I shall be back in the United
States in July when I shall conduct on the 28th at the Hollywood Ball [Bowl] in Los Angeles.

Looking forward to your news, I am sending you my very
affectionate remembrances

Cordially
Villa-Lobos

Adress in Europe: HOTEL BEDFORD
17 RUE DE L'ARCADE
PARIS – FRANCE

A little more than a month after the UNESCO concert Villa-
Lobos despatched a letter to Luiz Heitor Corrêa de Azevedo

---

[41] Apparently the third copy to be sent to Schwerké.

(1905–92), the Brazilian musicologist who, since 1947, had held an important position at UNESCO, where he exercised considerable influence on the International Music Council until his retirement in 1965.

In LETTER 56 Villa-Lobos mentions the outstanding success of the concerts he had organised to honour Florent Schmitt, in return for the help and support Schmitt had given him in Paris. Schmitt arrived in Brazil in September 1949 on the S. S. Kerguelen. A concert of his music was held on 31 October in the Municipal Theatre in Rio de Janeiro, and on the following day the Academia Brasileira de Música, founded by Villa-Lobos four years previously, honoured him with a reception and another concert in the building of the Brazilian Press Association. And on 4 November a Florent Schmitt Chamber Music Festival was held in the auditorium of the Ministry of Culture and Education. Shortly afterwards, Schmitt, only ten months away from his eightieth birthday, returned to Europe by boat.

LETTER 56
VILLA-LOBOS TO LUIZ HEITOR CORRÊA DE AZEVEDO
Original: Portuguese

Ministry of Education and Health

Rio, 6 November 1949

Mr. Luiz Heitor C. de Azevedo
UNESCO
19, Avenue Kleber-Paris 16 ème

My dear Luiz Heitor:

In reply to your kind letters of 19 and 21 October, I want to thank you for sending me the concert programme, very pretty, by the way, as well as the payment of my royalties.

I was surprised that the biographical data did not include my titles from the Institute of France and the Cross of Officer of the Légion d'Honneur in a programme organised in that country; isn't that so?

I will send you tomorrow, by airmail, two copies of 'Hommage à Chopin', already made known in Campos, Petropolis, Rio and, lately, in New York, with great success.

The idea of repeating the programme, in Rio, would be very interesting but difficult to realise, and you know very well yourself of the innumerable difficulties of organising something without money.

Just latterly, I have been working hard and, thank God, with excellent results on the programmes for my good friend, Florent Schmitt. I had the disinterested collaboration of various artists, and I confess to you, if it were not the great Florent, whom I hold in high esteem and for whom I feel grateful for having so early understood and respected me, I would not have proposed to organise myself the programme for which I had to solicit the free participation of professional artists.

Florent, who had a very good reception in Rio and was much feted, is already on his way back to Paris, delighted with our country and our people. He left amongst us a great number of friends. I feel much rewarded for all the work I put in because of the great pleasure rendered to such a great musician and friend.

Nice initiative, the commemoration of the Bach bi-centenary.

With our affectionate greetings to you two, a cordial embrace from

Villa-Lobos

R. Araujo Porto Alegre 56
Rio de Janeiro
Brazil

The last observable evidence of the mutual affection between Villa-Lobos and Schmitt is a letter from two years later.[42]

---

[42] It was published for the first time in Lisa M. Peppercorn, 'A Villa-Lobos Autograph Letter at the Bibliothèque Nationale (Paris)', *Latin American Music Review* (University of Texas Press, Austin) Vol. 1, No. 2, 1980, pp. 253–64.

LETTER 57
VILLA-LOBOS TO FLORENT SCHMITT AND HIS WIFE
Original: French

H. Villa-Lobos
R. Araujo Porto Alegre 56-Apto. 54
Rio de Janeiro
Brazil

Rio, 25 September 1951

Dear Friends:

It was a great pleasure for us to receive your letter, always welcome.

We were already worried without any news from the two of you. We don't know why the letters don't arrive.

We are very glad to know about the performances of works of our dear Florent and that they have the success they deserve.

Thank you very much for our dear Florent's kind letter. We hope to be together in February and it is a pity that we cannot go up the *Pão de Assucar* [43] with you two.

All friends here always remember you and they send you their affectionate remembrances.

It is a long time since I have seen Jean Français. [44] We were together many times with Mme. Mineur, [45] a charming woman, and so kind to us, and who has talked much about you.

In the hope of seeing you again soon, we embrace you cordially

Arminda and Villa-Lobos

Mr. Florent Schmitt
44 Quai du Passy
Paris-France

[43] The Sugar Loaf Mountain, which overlooks Rio de Janeiro.

[44] The French composer Jean Françaix (b. 1912).

[45] Gabrielle Mineur was for many years cultural attaché at the French embassy in Rio de Janeiro. A scientist by training, she married into the Brazilian Lage family.

PART IV
COMMISSIONS
AND CELEBRITY

Overleaf:
Villa-Lobos conducting the Philadelphia Orchestra, 22 January 1955
(courtesy of the Museu Villa-Lobos)

With three exceptions, all the letters Villa-Lobos is known to have written between 1951 and 1956 deal with commissions. In the last fifteen years of his life he fulfilled requests for 22 commissions, including two stage works, three ballets, seven concertos, six orchestral and two chamber works, one for piano solo, and a film score.

The first of these originated in a note from Aldo Parisot, the Brazilian cellist who, since 1946, has lived in the United States; he is currently on the faculty of the Yale School of Music and devotes his leisure hours to abstract paintings. He was born in Natal, Brazil, in 1918; after giving concerts all over the world – from the age of 12 – he eventually found the travelling tiresome and decided to devote his talents to teaching. Shortly before giving the US premieres (on 23 and 25 November 1951) of the *Fantasia* for cello and orchestra (composed in 1945) in a concert conducted by Stokowski, he raised a query from an orchestral trumpeter; Villa-Lobos' reply was characteristically colourful.

LETTER 58
VILLA-LOBOS TO ALDO PARISOT
Original: Portuguese

H. Villa-Lobos
R. Araujo Porto Alegre 56 – Apto. 54
Rio de Janeiro
Brazil

Rio de Janeiro, 15 November 1951

Dear Parisot:

Your letter of 27 October brought me much satisfaction with the pleasant news of your next performance in the United States under Stokowski. My congratulations and sincere wishes for good luck.

Regarding the information solicited about the mute cup, I would like you to explain to the trumpet player that, for many years in Brazil, the mute cup was a hat that covered on the side the instrument's bell to give a more veiled sound to prevent the police hearing the serenaders play at dawn in the streets. Today, however, there is the American 'mute cup' which is a perfect substitute for the system used by our popular players.

I must leave for the United States in the first fortnight of December. I shall stay at the New Weston Hotel until February, then I shall leave for Europe to give a series of concerts in various countries. In the United States, apart from conducting in Buffalo and Boston, I must settle my affairs with the Villa-Lobos Corporation,[1] the principal reason for my trip.

Hoping to see you again and to embrace you soon for another success, here is a cordial embrace from

Villa-Lobos

Mr Aldo Parisot
408 North Neville St.
Pittsburg, Pa.
USA

In 1953 Parisot commissioned Villa-Lobos to write a cello concerto for him. The result was only Villa-Lobos' second for the instrument, perhaps surprisingly, since it was the cello he played himself. (The first, his *Primeiro Grande Concerto de Violoncello*, Op. 50, was written in 1915 and premiered, by Newton de Menezes Pádua, in the Municipal Theatre in Rio de Janeiro on 10 May 1919.) The Concerto No. 2 for Violoncello and Orchestra was premiered by Parisot and the New York Philharmonic Symphony Orchestra on 5 February 1955, with Walter Hendl (born 1917) conducting.

[1] The Villa-Lobos Music Corporation, later renamed Consolidated Music Publishers, Inc., now functions from 24 East 22nd Street, New York, N.Y. 10010.

Villa-Lobos with Aldo Parisot, trying out parts of the Second Cello Concerto (courtesy of Irwin Dribben)

LETTER 59
VILLA-LOBOS TO ALDO PARISOT
Original: Portuguese

Rio de Janeiro, 26 October 1953

H. Villa-Lobos   Mr ALDO PARISOT
R. Araujo Porto Alegre 56 – Apt. 54   Wilton, CONN.
Rio de janeiro   USA
Brazil

Dear Parisot:

In reply to your kind letter of the 16th inst., I inform you that I shall have much pleasure in writing a work for you in accordance with the proposal presented, making for you the

H. VILLA·LOBOS
R. ARAUJO PORTO ALEGRE, 56 - APT. 54
RIO DE JANEIRO
BSASIL

Rio de Janeiro, 15 de Novembro de 1951

Prezado Parisot:

A sua carta de 27 de Outubro p.f,trouxe-me muita satisfação pela agradavel noticia de sua próxima apresentação nos Estados Unidos, sob a regência de Stoko wsky. Meus parabens e sinceros votos de felicidades.

Com referência à informação solicitada sobre a surdina copo, peço-lhe explicar ao trompetista que a surdina copo, há muitos anos usada no Brasil, era um chapéo que cobria do lado a campana do instrumento, afim de dar um som mais velado,para evitar que a policia ouvisse os seresteiros tocarem alta madrugada, nas ruas. Hoje,porém, há a surdina americana chamada " Mute Cup" que substitue perfeitamente o sistema usado pelos nossos tocadores populares.

Deverei partir para os Estados Unidos na primeira quinzena de Dezembro,onde ficarei hospedado no New-Westan Hotel até Fevereiro, quando partirei para a Europa, afim de realizar uma série de concertos em diversos países. Nos Estados Unidos, além de dirigir em Buffalo e Boston, deverei solucionar os meus negocios com a Villa-Lobos Corporation, motivo principal de minha viagem.

Esperando poder reve-lo e abraça-lo breve por mais outro sucesso, aqui vai o cordial abraço de

H.Villa-Lobos

Mr.Aldo Parisot
408 North Neville st.
Pittsburgh,Pa.
USA

Letter (58) to Aldo Parisot (courtesy of Aldo Parisot)

special concession of 2 years' exclusive use from the date of delivery of the orchestral score, something, by the way, I have not done before for any other artists. Thus, you will have a longer period to present the work with the orchestras in the United States.

Regarding the Letter-Contract, you can draw it up yourself, in the United States and send it directly to Rio and I shall return one of the copies to you duly signed.

Now, here is the answer to your kind wife: when can a father say that the 'Son' will be this or that? Now then, I don't know what will come out of my pen and thus it will be impossible for me to make any promise about the Concerto for Violoncello and Orchestra.

The only thing I can declare is that I shall write a work with sincerity; it remains to be seen, nevertheless, if this sincerity will please or not.

With our longings for the TRIO,[2] a cordial embrace from

H. Villa-Lobos

On 25 October 1983 Aldo Parisot wrote to me in response to an earlier letter of mine. Part of his letter gives a fascinating glimpse of Villa-Lobos' composing methods – and of the speed at which he worked:

He wrote the Concerto in New York in 1954.[3] I used to go every day, for one week, to his hotel in New York and practise in his apartment. He asked me to play scales, etudes, sonatas, concertos etc. so he could hear my playing and write a work that was tailor made, so to speak. I remember that while he was writing passages of the Concerto he would show them to me and ask me to try them. Many times he would remark 'no,' try this way' and would pick up the cello and demonstrate to me how he wanted the passage played. As you know, he was a cellist. One interesting fact is that while he was composing the Concerto he was also writing a Symphony at the same time and would switch from one work to the other.[4] If I remember correctly, he finished the concerto in one week. After every session in the morning we took a rest. Arminda would cook delicious feijoada[5] for us and Villa-Lobos would tell many funny Brazilian jokes.

[2] The 'trio' consisted of Aldo Parisot's three sons (letter to me from Aldo Parisot, dated 15 August 1989).

[3] A slip: the Concerto was composed in 1953, as the first page of the manuscript (*cf.* p. 140) confirms.

[4] None of Villa-Lobos' Symphonies dates from 1953 or 1954; the work in question may have been another orchestral piece.

[5] A Brazilian national dish of black beans and rice.

H. VILLA-LOBOS
R. Araujo Porto Alegre, 56 - Apt. 54   Rio de Janeiro, 26 de outubro de 1953
Rio de Janeiro
Brasil

                    Mr.ALDO PARISOT
                    Wilton,CONN.
                    USA

        Prezado Parisot:

        Em resposta à sua estimada carta de 16 do corrente, comunico-lhe que
terei muito prazer em escrever uma obra para V., de acôrdo com a propos-
ta apresentada, fazendo a concessão especial de dar a exclusividade de 2
anos, a partir da data da entrega da partitura da Orquestra, o que aliás
não fiz ainda com nenhum artista. Assim,ficará V. com um prazo maior para
apresentação da obra com as Orquestras, nos Estados Unidos.

        Com referência à Carta-Contrato, V. mesmo poderá faze-la,nos Estados
Unidos e envia-la dirétamente ao Rio e uma das cópias remeterei a V. de-
vidamente assinada.

        Agora, aqui vai a resposta à sua simpática Esposa: Quando é que um
pai poderá dizer que o "Filho" será tal ou qual? Pois é, nada sei sobre
o que virá da minha pena, e por isso ser-me-à impossivel fazer alguma
promessa sobre o Concerto de Violoncelo e Orquestra.

        A única cousa que poderei afirmar é que escreverei uma obra com sin-
ceridade, restando saber, no entanto, se essa sinceridade poderá ou não
agradar.

        Com as nossas saudades ao TRIO, o cordial abraço do

                            H.Villa-Lobos

Letter (59) to Aldo Parisot (courtesy of Aldo Parisot)

Bernardo Segáll (born in 1911), the distinguished Brazilian pianist currently on the faculty of the University of Southern California,
was hailed by the critics as the 'undisputed find of the season' after
his New York debut, in the Town Hall on 27 December 1936.
He is also active as a composer, having provided the scores for
Broadway productions of Tennessee Williams' *Campino Real* and

William Saroyan's *Cave Dwellers* and a variety of plays in Los
Angeles, as well as for several ballets produced in the Lincoln
Center and for a number of films. But it was as a pianist that, in
1952, he commissioned Villa-Lobos to write a work for him. Villa-
Lobos responded in the same year with his Piano Concerto No. 4.
There are no surviving documents relating to this commission; in
Bernardo Segáll's own words:[6]

> In 1976 my house in the Malibu fire was burned down and
> with it all my manuscripts, letters, reviews etc. All I
> remember of Villa-Lobos correspondence on the Concerto are
> reports of its progress from Rio, then Paris, where he finished
> the second movement. He finished it in New York in 1952. I
> was then living in N.Y. He conducted my performances of
> the Concerto with the Pittsburgh[7] and L. A. Philharmonic
> which was performed at the Hollywood Bowl. I performed it
> with the N.Y. Philharmonic under Leonard Bernstein. I also
> performed [it] in Rio & S. Paulo under Eleazar de Carvalho.

The correspondence between Villa-Lobos and the Louisville Orchestra is self-explanatory. The commission discussed in this
exchange was the second commission that Villa-Lobos had received
from the Orchestra. The first was requested in 1950, after a decision by the Orchestra in the spring of 1948 'instead of engaging
expensive soloists [...] using the budget for soloists to "commission" composers of world renown to write pieces especially for the
Orchestra'.[8] Villa-Lobos responded to the first commission with
Erosão (Erosion), a symphonic poem based on a legend of the 'Origin of the Amazon River', collected by João Barbosa Rodrigues

6 In a letter to me, dated 6 May 1984.

7 The premiere and repeat performance, on 9 and 11 January 1953.

8 Robert Sutton Whitney (1904–86), conductor of the Louisville Orchestra, in his *The Louisville Orchestra*, published by the Orchestra, no date,
p. 9. The composers commissioned for the 1948–49 season, for example,
were Darius Milhaud, Virgil Thomson, Roy Harris, Joaquin Rodrigo, Gian
Francesco Malipiero and Claude Almand (a Louisville composer); for the
following season commissions were received by Paul Hindemith, William
Schuman, David Diamond, Robert Russell Bennett and Claude Almand.

Manuscript first page of the Second Cello Concerto
(courtesy of Éditions Max Eschig)

(1842–1909).[9] The Louisville Orchestra has no correspondence concerning *Erosão*,[10] which it premiered under the baton of Robert Whitney on 7 and 8 November 1951.

Villa-Lobos responded to the second commission with an overture, *Alvorada na Floresta Tropical (Dawn in a Tropical Forest)*, first performed in a recording studio (for the Orchestra's own label, First Edition Records) on 23 January 1954.

Villa-Lobos had meantime left his concert agent, Henri Leiser, choosing instead the formidable Arthur Judson[11] of Columbia Artists Management, as the last three letters in this exchange (LETTERS 69–71) reveal.

LETTER 60
R. H. WANGERIN TO VILLA-LOBOS
Original: English

July 22, 1953

Mr. Heitor Villa-Lobos
c/o Mr. Milton Peterson
120 West 70th Street
New York 23, New York

Dear Mr. Villa-Lobos,

As of January 1, 1954 the Louisville Orchestra will inaugurate a series of 46 weekly programs of new music. One new

---

[9] *Cf.* note 23 on p. 100. The legend which inspired the symphonic poem is retold, in French, in *Mythes, Contes et Légendes des Indiens: Folklore Brésilien* (A. Ferroud-F. Ferroud, Paris, 1930), by Gustavo Dodt Barroso (1888–1959), the first director of the Historical Museum in Rio de Janeiro. The symphonic poem reflects the legend's themes of the Andes Mountains, the Amazon valley, and the creation of the River Amazon.

[10] According to a letter to me from Gerald Dolter, Public Relations Assistant of the Louisville Orchestra, dated 25 March 1981.

[11] Judson (1881–1975) trained as a violinist, was manager of the Philadelphia Orchestra from 1915 to 1935 and of the New York Philharmonic Orchestra from 1922 until his resignation in 1956; he was also president of the Columbia Concerts Corporation from 1930, and later a member of the board of directors of Columbia Artists Management. This combination of positions made him one of the most powerful men in the musical life of North America.

commissioned work will be introduced each week and repeated for three subsequent weeks. Selected works will then be recorded to be released in a monthly series and distributed under our own label on an annual subscription basis. During the five seasons we have been commissioning new music our works have varied in length from five to around twenty minutes. We would like to offer you a commission and to have you feel free to make your work of any length you choose within that span.

Your piece may be for orchestra alone. But if you contemplate a work using soloists or choral participation we wish to be informed in advance so we may judge the practicability of such participation in terms of our resources here. We have an orchestra of 50 players with the following instrumentation:

> 2 flutes (doubling piccolos), 2 oboes (1 doubles English horn), 2 clarinets, 2 bassoons, 4 horns, 2 trumpets, 3 trombones, tuba, timpani, 1 percussion, harp, optional piano and strings, 9–8–6–5–4.

Any other instruments must be optional.

If you write the work for us it is agreed that in the event it is published it will carry an acknowledgement, if not a dedication to the effect that the work was commissioned by the Louisville Orchestra and given its world premiere performance in Louisville.

The Louisville Orchestra is prepared to offer you a commission of $1,000.00. The orchestra parts must be furnished by you and we are making a blanket allowance of $200.00 additional to assist you in getting this task completed. Payment will be made upon performance or within 90 days of receipt whichever is earlier. This sum will entitle us to performance rights and use of the orchestral material for six performances. We would also like to request two copies of the score, one copy to remain in our library, the other returned to you or your publisher.

If the work is recorded we agree to pay you a royalty of three cents ($0.03) per record on each record sold by us on our label.

Bernardo Segáll
(courtesy of Irving
Bazelon)

It is our hope that you will compose a work for us: the score and parts to be delivered to us by February 1, 1954. We realize that this is extremely short notice. If the date is not feasible, please inform us by August 21st what you think would be the earliest practicable delivery date.

Sincerely yours

R.H. Wangerin

Secretary to Commissioning Committee

The Pittsburgh Symphony Orchestra

WILLIAM STEINBERG, Conducting
HEITOR VILLA-LOBOS, Guest Conductor
BERNARDO SEGALL, Piano Soloist

SYRIA MOSQUE

Friday Evening, January 9, 1953
Sunday Afternoon, January 11, 1953

PROGRAM

Villa-Lobos .... Choros No. 6

Villa-Lobos .... Concerto No. 4 for Piano and Orchestra*
    Allegro non troppo
    Andante con moto
    Scherzo — Allegro vivace
    Allegro moderato — Lento — Allegro moderato
            Mr. Segall

        Both Works Under the Direction of the Composer

INTERMISSION

Schumann .... Symphony No. 1 in B-flat major, Op. 38
    Andante un poco maestoso
    Larghetto
    Molto vivace
    Allegro animato e grazioso

*UNITED STATES PREMIERE

STEINWAY PIANOS   CAPITOL RECORDS
                            (13)

Programme of the US premiere of the Fourth Piano Concerto

LETTER 61
VILLA-LOBOS TO R. H. WANGERIN
Original: French[12]

Rio de Janeiro
August 16, 1953

Mr. R. H. Wangerin, Secretary
Commissioning Committee
The Louisville Orchestra
830 South 4th Street
Louisville, Kentucky

Dear Mr. Wangerin:
In response to your letter of July 22, I want to tell you that I agree to your proposition concerning my writing a work to be commissioned by the Louisville Orchestra.

The work will be approximately 12 to 14 minutes in length, and will be written for the orchestra without a soloist.

I hope to send you the parts and the orchestra material around the first of February, 1954.

Best regards,

H. Villa-Lobos

LETTER 62
R. H. WANGERIN TO VILLA-LOBOS
Original: English

September 4, 1953

Mr. H. Villa-Lobos
R. Araujo Porto Alegre, 56
Apt. 54
Rio de Janeiro, Brazil

Dear Mr. Villa-Lobos:
We are more than pleased to learn that you have accepted our commission and look forward to receiving the score and

---

[12] According to a letter to me from Gerald Dolter, dated 4 May 1981, 'the letter dated 16 Aug. 1953 was missing in its original form. I regret that all that was in the file was the translation'.

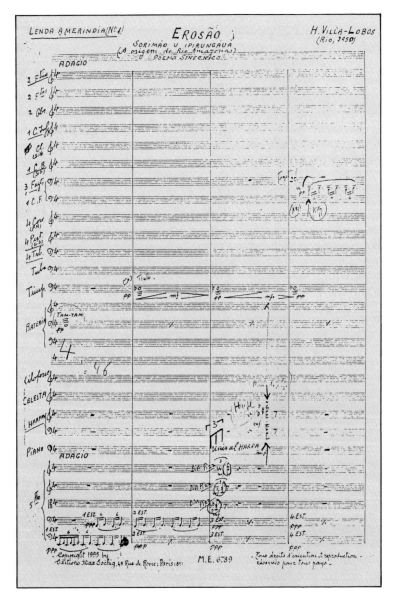

Manuscript first page of Alvorada na Floresta Tropical
(*courtesy of Éditions Max Eschig*)

parts by February, 1954, and to hearing your work when it is performed.

With every good wish,

> Sincerely yours,
> R.H. Wangerin
> Secretary to
> Commission Recommendation Committee.

LETTER 63
VILLA-LOBOS TO R. H. WANGERIN
Original: French

H. Villa-Lobos
R. Araujo Porto Alegre, 56 – Apt. 54
Rio de janeiro
Brazil

Rio de Janeiro, 8 November, 1953

> Mr. R.H. WANGERIN
> Secretary to Commissioning Committee
> The Louisville Orchestra
> 830 South 4th Street
> Louisville, Kentucky

Dear Sir:

I have the pleasure of sending you the score (2 copies) of 'DAWN IN A TROPICAL FOREST' (ALVORADA NA FLORESTA TROPICAL) – Overture, the work which I have written under commission by 'The Louisville Orchestra'.

I will send you the orchestral material at the very beginning of December.

Hoping that the orchestra will be glad, I take this opportunity to send you my most cordial greetings.

[unsigned[13]]

---

[13] According to *ibid.*, 'VL's signature was missing at the bottom in the original'.

Manuscript first page of Alvorada na Floresta Tropical
(courtesy of Éditions Max Eschig)

LETTER 64
R. H. WANGERIN TO VILLA-LOBOS
Original: English

November 28, 1953

Mr. H. Villa-Lobos
R. Araujo Porto Alegre, 56 – Apt. 54
Rio de Janeiro, Brazil

Dear Mr. Villa-Lobos:

We have received the two scores of your 'Dawn in a Tropical Forest' and look forward to receiving the parts and performing the work. Thank you and with best wishes.

Sincerely yours

R.H. Wangerin
Secretary to
Commission Recommendation Committee

LETTER 65
VILLA-LOBOS TO LOUISE TACHAU
Original: English

Hollywood Knickerbocker Hotel
Hollywood

Los Angeles, January,
17th, 1954

Miss Louise Tachau
Assistant to the Manager
Louisville Philharmonic Society
830 South Fourth Street
Louisville 3, KY

Dear Miss Tachau:

I just received your letter of December 22th sent to Brasil and I am very glad to present you some words about 'Dawn in a Tropical Forest'.

'A dawn, in any tropical forest of Brazil, is for me an *overture* of colors accompanied by the magic singing and chirping of the tropical birds, and also by howls, squeals, evocations and the exotic and barbaric dances of the native Indians.

The 'Dawn in a Tropical forest' is written based in the same musical form used in Beethoven's overtures, but with less thematic and developing.

The themes of this work are original and they are treating in the certains scales brazilian indiens.

If you have some other questions, can you write to 'NEW ANTILLA HOTEL CORPORATION – Ponce de Leon Boulevard in Coral Gables–Florida.

With my best wishes,

H. Villa-Lobos

LETTER 66
R. H. WANGERIN TO VILLA-LOBOS
Original: English

January 21, 1954

Mr. Heitor Villa-Lobos
New Antilla Hotel Corporation
Ponce de Leon Boulevard
Coral Gables, Florida

Dear Mr. Villa-Lobos:

Thank you so much for your prompt reply giving us comments on your 'Dawn in a Tropical Forest'. We have scheduled the first performance of this work for this coming Saturday, January 23rd with subsequent performances on Saturdays, February 6th and 13th and March 6th.

I was wondering whether you wanted us to send your check to you at the Coral Gables address, and whether there is any chance you might be planning to be present for one of the performances. Naturally we would be more than honoured if you would see your way clear to pay us a visit.

We are looking forward very much to hearing your work performed. With every good wish.

Sincerely yours
R.H. Wangerin
Manager

LETTER 67
VILLA-LOBOS TO R. H. WANGERIN
Original: English

New Antilla
On Ponce de Leon Boulevard
Coral Gables, Florida

Coral Gables, 4 February 1954

Mr. R. H. Wangerin
THE LOUISVILLE ORCHESTRA

Dear Mr. Wangerin:

In reply your letter of January 21st, I inform you that you can send the check to NEW WESTON HOTEL (Madison Av. at 50th St – New-York) where I must arrive next 16th.

Unfortunately it will be impossible to me to be present for one of the performances of my 'Dawn in a Tropical Forest', but my wife will be very happy if you can send her the program and review, because she likes to collect everything about my music.

Hoping the LOUISVILLE ORCHESTRA will be glad with my Overture, I send you my best wishes,

Cordially
H. Villa-Lobos

LETTER 68
R. H. WANGERIN TO VILLA-LOBOS
Original: English

February 15, 1954

Mr. H. Villa-Lobos
New Weston Hotel
Madison Ave. at 50th Street
New York, New York

Dear Mr. Villa-Lobos:

As per your instructions I am enclosing your check for $1200.00, payment in full for the commissioning fee and allowance for copying of parts as agreed upon.

We are very sorry you couldn't be present for one of the performances. I am also enclosing copies of the program and press review. The work was well received by the audience. With every good wish.

Sincerely yours
R.H. Wangerin
Manager

LETTER 69
VILLA-LOBOS TO R. H. WANGERIN
Original: English

Hotel New Weston
Madison Ave. at Fiftieth St.
New York 22, N.Y.

New York, 5 march 1955

Mr. R.H. WANGERIN
The Louisville Orchestra
830 South Fourth Street
Louisville 3, Kentucky

Dear Mr. Wangerin:
    I am very glad to write you to inform you that next season (december to february), I must conduct concerts in some cities very near of Louisville and I would like to know if you think it would be possible to me to be guest conductor of your Orchestra.
    This season I have the great honour to be invited to conduct one tour with Philadelphia Orchestra with a program with my own works and we are very happy.
    In the case you give me the excellent opportunity to conduct your very good Orchestre that I had the great pleasure

Villa-Lobos on 18 May 1955, in front of the restaurant L'Acropole in Paris, where he used to take his daily meals, often with guests he had invited, when he was visiting the French capital; L'Acropole was opposite the Hotel Bedford, in the rue de l'Arcade, where he kept a permanent room from 1952. In his room was put the writing desk of Pedro II, Emperor of Brazil from 1840 until 1889 (courtesy of Luiz Heitor Corrêa de Azevedo).

to hear to play my Erosion and Down in a tropical forest,[14] please write my manager, Mr. Arthur Judson (Columbia Concerts).

With my best wishes,
H. Villa-Lobos

My adresse in Europe until july – HOTEL BEDFORD
17 rue de l'Arcade
Paris – France

[14] Presumably on the recordings made by the Louisville Orchestra.

LETTER 70
VILLA-LOBOS TO R. H. WANGERIN
Original: English

January 21th, 1956

Hotel New Weston
Madison Avenue at 50th Street
New York 22, N.Y.

Mr. R.H. WANGERIN, MANAGER
The LOUISVILLE ORCHESTRA
830 South Fourth Street
Louisville 3, Kentucky

Dear Mr. Wangerin:

I am beginning to set my plans for next season and it would be very nice if I could know if your kind idea of having me in The Louisville will be possible. It would be a great honor and pleasure for me to conduct your celebrated orchestra. My business affairs are in the hands of Mr. Arthur Judson and Mr. Bruno Zirato and they have my available dates. I shall appreciate it greatly if you will let me or them know what you have in mind for me.

With most cordial greetings to Mr. Whitney and to you, I remain

Yours sincerely
H. Villa-Lobos

LETTER 71
R. H. WANGERIN TO ARTHUR JUDSON
Original: English

February 8, 1956
Mr. Arthur Judson
Columbia Artists Management, Inc.
113 West 57th Street
New York 19, New York

Dear Mr. Judson:

We recently received a letter from Mr. Villa-Lobos which gives me the impression that he believes we are interested in booking him as a guest conductor.

*Villa-Lobos with Luiz Heitor Corrêa de Azevedo (1905–92),
photographed on the composer's only visit to the Paris headquarters of
UNESCO, on 15 June 1956 (courtesy of UNESCO)*

For your information, some years ago there was correspondence with him about the possibility of his conducting the world premiere performance of a work we had commissioned him to write. Both of the works we commissioned him to do have long since been performed and recorded and we are not in a position to hire any guest conductor at the moment.

Best wishes.

Sincerely yours

R.H. Wangerin
Manager

For five months in 1954 Villa-Lobos corresponded with Janet Collins (b. 1917), the American dancer who was *première danseuse* at the Metropolitan Opera House in New York from 1951 to 1954; after her retirement she taught dance for a while before devoting herself to painting. The work that resulted from her commission was the ballet, *Genesis*. In LETTER 59 Villa-Lobos had told Aldo

Parisot that he had never granted a two-year period of exclusivity to any other artist; he was now to award the same privilege to Janet Collins. She choreographed *Genesis*, though she did not dance in it herself.[15] In her words:[16]

> The theme of Genesis is God's creation of man – the man's evolving consciousness into complete awareness of his Creator [...]. Villa-Lobos wrote the work from a detailed dance libretto I wrote for him [...]. The work was composed for a dance soloist with full symphonic form. I am only familiar with the duo-piano version – which in itself is a small masterpiece! It is beautiful music – and worthy of this great Brazilian composer.

LETTER 72
VILLA-LOBOS TO JANET COLLINS
Original: French

New Antilla Hotel
On Ponce de Leon Boulevard
In Coral Gables, Florida

Miss JANET COLLINS
164 West 88 Street
New-York   Miami, 9 February, 1954

Dear Miss Collins,
I have just received your letter of 29 January, sent to Brazil, it gives me pleasure to reply.

I am interested in the idea of your scenario for a ballet with my music but I ask you if you know some of my works well, as, for instance, the music which was recorded for: EROSÃO: Origin of the Amazon River – UIRAPURU – NONETTO – CHÔROS IV, VII AND X, CIRANDAS, QUARTETO No. 6 etc. If you are not, I think it would be good if you could hear them and in this way have a contact with some of my work and be sure that the music appeals to your temperament.

[15] Its concert premiere took place on 21 November 1969, ten years to the month after Villa-Lobos' death, in the Teatro Municipal in Rio de Janeiro.

[16] In an undated letter to me from Seattle, postmarked 3 April 1981.

I need to know the instrumentation, the length of the ballet and I also inform you that my conditions are, at least, the following: $1,000 dollars at the signing of a letter-contract; $1,000 dollars on the presentation of the work; exclusivity 2 (two) years.

If you agree with my conditions, I think it best if you could meet me in New-York (NEW WESTON HOTEL – Madison Av. at 50th Street) where I shall be from the 16th until the end of February.

With my thanks for your interest in my music.

Yours sincerely
H. Villa-Lobos

LETTER 73
VILLA-LOBOS TO JANET COLLINS
Original: French

Miss Janet Collins   Paris, 5 May, 1954
c/o Frank R. La Briola
New-York – N.Y.

Dear Miss Collins,

I am pleased to send your Ballet GENESIS, the orchestral score and the reduction for piano, according to our agreement in New-York.

I take advantage of this opportunity to tell you that my instrumentation can be for a full orchestra of 64 or more musicians and for a small orchestra of 24 as you can see from the enclosed list.

I shall try to have a private recording done of the reduction . for piano and I shall send it to you as soon as it is ready.

Looking forward to your news, my wife and myself send you our affectionate remembrances and good luck with your Ballet.

Cordially
H. Villa-Lobos

HOTEL BEDFORD
17 rue de l'Arcade
Paris – France

Manuscript first page of Genesis *(courtesy of Éditions Max Eschig)*

LETTER 74
VILLA-LOBOS TO JANET COLLINS
Original: French

Paris, 31 May, 1954

Miss JANET COLLINS
164 West 88 Street
New-York 24, N.Y.

Dear Miss Collins,

It was a great pleasure for me to have received your news and to know that you are satisfied with your GENESIS.

I am about to arrange a recording with two pianists and as soon as it is ready, I shall send it to you immediately.

I am sure you will be much happier after you have heard the music with orchestra, because it has more colours which the piano cannot produce.

I don't know if you have noticed that I made an orchestration for full orchestra and small orchestra, but I think if you shall have the opportunity to do the world premiere with a full orchestra this would be better for the work and for you.

When do you intend to dance it? I should be very glad to have the opportunity of applauding you and I am convinced that you will have a great success with your great talent.

Mr. Frank Briola[17] has already been in touch with me about your cheque.

With very affectionate remembrances from my wife and myself

Cordially

H. Villa-Lobos

Rua Araujo Porto Alegre 56, Apt. 54
RIO DE JANEIRO
BRAZIL

---

[17] Unidentified; presumably Janet Collins' agent.

LETTER 75
VILLA-LOBOS TO JANET COLLINS
Original: French

Paris, 2 July, 1954

Miss JANET COLLINS
164 West 88th Street
NEW YORK 24, N.Y.

Dear Miss Collins,
As I had promised you I have sent you, by air, the recording in 'tape' of your ballet GENESIS.
Unfortunately it is not very good except for the rhythm and the movements because the recording place was very bad.
In spite of many difficulties in finding equipment to make this recording, I am very glad to have succeeded with this.
I hope it will be of use to you and I beg you to send me a copy for myself to my address at RUA ARAUJO PORTO ALEGRE 56 – RIO DE JANEIRO – BRAZIL.
Wishing you the best, my wife and myself send you our affectionate remembrances

H. Villa-Lobos

RUA ARAUJO PORTO ALEGRE 56
RIO DE JANEIRO
BRAZIL

Later that year, 1954, Villa-Lobos received a letter from the Boston Symphony Orchestra as one of several composers around the world commissioned to write a work to celebrate the Orchestra's 75th anniversary in the 1955–56 season.[18] He responded with his Eleventh Symphony, dedicated to the memory of Natalie and Serge Koussevitzky.[19]

[18] The other composers commissioned for these celebrations were Samuel Barber, Leonard Bernstein, Aaron Copland, Henri Dutilleux, Gottfried von Einem, Howard Hanson, Jacques Ibert (who undertook to compose a symphony but died after completing the first movement), Darius Milhaud, Goffredo Petrassi, Walter Piston, William Schuman and Roger Sessions (letter from Jane E. Ward, Archival Assistant to the Boston Symphony Orchestra, dated 22 February 1989).

[19] Natalie Koussevitzky had died in 1942 and her husband nine years later.

MUSEU VILLA-LOBOS (Palacio da Cultura)
Sexta-feira 21 de novembro, as 17,30 horas

LANÇAMENTO DO DISCO: PIANO DE VILLA-LOBOS -- ARNALDO ESTRELLA
E DAS PUBLICAÇÕES.' PRESENÇA DE VILLA-LOBOS (4° volume) e
COMENTARIOS SÔBRE A OBRA PIANISTICA DE VILLA-
LOBOS por SOUZA LIMA

TEATRO   MUNICIPAL
Sexta-feira, 21 de novembro, às 21 horas

MARIO TAVARES, regente

PRELÚDIO E FUGA N.º 6 de J. S. Bach (Transcrição para orquestra de Villa-Lobos)

GÊNESIS (Poema Sinfônico e Bailado) (1954)
1.ª audição mundial

FLORESTA DO AMAZONAS (do filme Green Mansions) (1958)
MARIA LUCIA GODOY, solista
1.ª audição mundial (integral)

ORQUESTRA E CÔRO DO TEATRO MUNICIPAL
Maestros do Côro: HENRIQUE MORELENBAUN e NELSON NILO HACK

Programme of the premiere of Genesis, *in the Teatro Municipal,
Rio de Janeiro.*

LETTER 76
CHARLES MUNCH *ET AL.* TO VILLA-LOBOS
Original: English

Boston Symphony Orchestra
Symphony Hall, Boston 15, Massachusetts

October 29, 1954

Mr. Heitor Villa-Lobos
Villa-Lobos Music Corporation
221 West 47th Street
New York, New York

Dear Mr. Villa-Lobos:

The Boston Symphony Orchestra will observe its 75th
Anniversary during the season 1955-56. To celebrate the
occasion, the Serge Koussevitzky Music Foundation in the

Library of Congress and the Boston Symphony Orchestra jointly are inviting a number of the leading composers of the United States, Europe and South America to accept commissions to compose works for the Orchestra. The Foundation and the Orchestra wish to invite you to accept one of these commissions to take part in the celebration.

The conditions of the commission are outlined on the attached sheet. If you accept, please sign the enclosed copy of this letter and return it to the Boston Symphony Orchestra, Symphony Hall, Boston 15, Mass. by December 1, 1954. Upon receipt of your acceptance, the initial check of $ 1,000 will be sent to you. Your acceptance of the commission implies acceptance of the conditions on the attached sheet.

The Foundation and the Orchestra will be much honored if you are free to undertake this work which we believe will constitute an important addition to the contemporary orchestral repertoire.

Faithfully yours

For the Boston Symphony Orchestra:
CHARLES MUNCH, Music Director
HENRY B. CABOT, President
MRS. SERGE KOUSSEVITZKY
Chairman, Advisory Board

For the Serge Koussevitzky
Music Foundation in the
Library of Congress:

I accept this commission:
[signed]
HEITOR VILLA-LOBOS   Date: November 29th, 1954

Early in 1955 Villa-Lobos was asked for his autograph by Claire Raphael Reis (1889–1978), a prominent figure in American musical circles. She was a founding member of The League of Composers in 1923, and chairman of its board for 25 years; she was also co-founder and, for ten years, chairman of the People's Music League, which presented concerts free of charge. She was also involved in

Villa-Lobos composing in his New York hotel, 1956
(courtesy of the Museu Villa-Lobos, Rio de Janeiro)

several other cultural organisations, and author of two books: *Composers, Conductors and Critics*[20] and *Composers in America*,[21] a reference work which included short biographies of living composers.

LETTER 77
VILLA-LOBOS TO CLAIRE REIS
Original: French

New York, 12 February, 1955

Mme Arthur Reis
99 East Seventh Ninth Street
New York, N.Y.

Hotel New Weston
Madison Avenue at 50th Street
New York, 22, N.Y.

Dear Madam,
    In reply to your kind letter of 7 February, I inform you that I have much pleasure to send you my autograph.
    Hoping to meet you in Brazil,

Cordially

H. Villa-Lobos

    In the autumn of that year, 1955, Villa-Lobos was approached by Guillermo Espinosa (born in 1905), then head of the Music Division of the Pan American Union in Washington, a post he held from 1952 to 1975.[22] I have been unable to discover what the project discussed in the letter was and what were Villa-Lobos' comments about it.

[20] Oxford University Press, New York, 1955 (2nd impr., Detroit Reprints in Music, Detroit, 1974).

[21] Macmillan, New York, 1938, 2nd edn. 1947; re-issued by Da Capo Press, New York, 1977.

[22] Born in Colombia, Espinosa studied music in Milan and Berlin. He was a guest conductor of orchestras in Italy, Switzerland, Denmark and France before founding the National Symphony Orchestra in Bogotá; he conducted it for ten years before settling in Washington.

LETTER 78
VILLA-LOBOS TO GUILLERMO ESPINOSA
Original: Portuguese

8 September 1955

Ministry of Education and Culture

Dr. Guillermo Espinosa
Chief, Music Division
of the Pan American Union
Washington 6, D.C. – U.S.A.

Dear friend:

Acknowledging and thanking you for the receipt of your esteemed note of 26/8/1955, concerning the cultural exchange project, conceived by the composer David Van Vactor,[23] I inform you that I await correspondence from the author of the project until the end of next November to have the pleasure of expressing my opinion of it.

With cordial greetings, I am always your friend and at your service,

H. Villa-Lobos

Three years later, in 1958, Villa-Lobos was invited to participate in the First Inter-American Music Festival, presented in Washington on 18–20 April under the auspices of the Pan American

---

[23] David Van Vactor (born in 1906) completed his studies in the United States before spending some time (1929–31) in Europe; he studied composition in Vienna with Franz Schmidt and with Paul Dukas in Paris, where he also studied flute with Marcel Moyse. Upon his return he joined the Chicago Symphony Orchestra as a flautist (1931–43); he taught theory at Northwestern University (1935–47), was head of the Department of Fine Arts at the University of Tennessee (1947–52) and professor of composition there (1947–77). He made three tours of South America as a member of the North American Woodwind Quintet, under the auspices of the State Department; he also has a reputation as a conductor, and was conductor of the Knoxville Symphony Orchestra from 1947 to 1972. His extensive list of compositions includes eight symphonies, several concertos, and much other orchestral music, as well as much vocal, chamber and instrumental music.

*Claire Raphael Reis
(1889–1978) at the
age of 62,
photographed by her
daughter Hilda
Bijur (courtesy of
Hilda Bijur)*

Union and organised by Guillermo Espinosa.[24] Among the works
presented in this first festival, Villa-Lobos' String Quartet No. 15
and Symphony No. 12 were world premieres. The Symphony had
been completed a year earlier, on 5 March 1957, the day of Villa-
Lobos' seventieth birthday. The Quartet was first performed by the
Juilliard String Quartet on 19 April, in the Coolidge Auditorium of
the Library of Congress. On the following day there was a concert
at noon that included two of Villa-Lobos' songs: *Cantos de Çairé*

[24] The Inter-American Music Festivals (1958–74), which Espinosa
founded and directed, presented 94 premieres of Latin American works in
six festivals. On 24 April 1961, during the second Inter-American Music
Festival (22–30 April), he conducted the National Symphony Orchestra of
Washington in the world premiere of Villa-Lobos' Ninth Symphony and
the American premiere of his Harmonica Concerto; the soloist was the
American virtuoso John Sebastian (1914–80), and the works were
presented in the Cramton Auditorium of Howard University in a 'Brazilian
Night' in homage to Villa-Lobos.

and *Invocação em Defesa da Patria*, performed by the Howard University Choir conducted by Warner Lawson. And that night, in the Lisner Auditorium, Howard Mitchell[25] conducted the National Symphony Orchestra in the premiere of the Symphony. The catalogue mentioned in Villa-Lobos' reply to Espinosa's report was probably destined for the series produced by the Pan American Union on *Composers of the Americas*. The Villa-Lobos article, written by Carleton Sprague Smith and Marcos Romero, appeared in Vol. 3, 1960, pp. 1–59; it was a reprint of an earlier (1957) edition and, strangely, did not include the works in the list Villa-Lobos sent to Espinosa.

LETTER 79
GUILLERMO ESPINOSA TO VILLA-LOBOS
Original: Spanish

Pan American Union

1 May 1958

My dear Master:

I wish to congratulate you most effusively on the notable success of your Quartet No. 15 and your Symphony No. 12 at the Festival in Washington. All your friends here regretted deeply that you could not be present. The Juilliard Quartet gave an excellent performance of your Quartet No. 15 and the Washington Symphony Orchestra one no less notable of your symphony. When you pass through New York, I will personally give you the press clippings.

I hope we will have the honour of counting on your valuable collaboration in the next Festival. We thought to include in the programme a short opera by a Latin American composer and another by one from the United States. All this was already discussed in the Programme Committee and all

[25] Born in 1911, Mitchell studied piano and trumpet before transferring his allegiances to the cello, which he studied at Peabody Conservatory in Baltimore and then the Curtis Institute in Philadelphia, as a student of Felix Salmond. He was principal cellist of the National Symphony Orchestra in Washington (1933–46), associate conductor (1946–49) and principal conductor (1949–70), before being nominated conductor of the National Orchestra of Uruguay.

MINISTÉRIO DA EDUCAÇÃO E SAÚDE

Em 8 de setembro de 1955.

Ilmo. Sr.
Dr. Guillermo Espinosa
DD. Chefe da Seção Musical
da União Panamericana
Washington 6, D. C. - E.U.A.

Prezado amigo:

Acusando e agradecendo o recebimen-
to de sua estimada cartinha de 26|9|1955,a res
peito do projeto de intercâmbio cultural ela -
borado pelo compositor David Van Vactor, comu-
nico-lhe que aguardo a correspondência do au -
tor do projeto, até fins de novembro próximo ,
a fim de ter o prazer de poder externar a mi -
nha opinião sôbre o mesmo.

Com as minhas saudações cordiais,dis
ponha do sempre amigo,

H. Villa-Lobos

*Letter (78) from Villa-Lobos to Guillermo Espinosa
(courtesy of the Organization of American States)*

its members are of the opinion that nobody but you would be
more qualified with your customary luxurious way of composing to realise such a lyrical work. Do you plan to write an
opera soon?

It gives me pleasure to tell you that one of the most emo-
tional moments of the Festival was when the famous choir of
the Howard University interpreted your *Invocação em Defesa
da Patria*. What a sublime moment. Everybody applauded

Lista de obras de H.Villa-Lobos

1957

1957 - MENINA DAS NU VENS - Opera comica(Aventura musical) -Argumento de Lucia Be-
em 3 átos - duração 2 hs. nedetti.

1957 - POEMA DE PALAVRAS - Canto e Piano ou Orquestra - Sobre a poesia " Histo-
- 4 minutos de duração - rietas" de Dora Vascon-
cellos.

1958 - FANTASIA CONCERTANTE Orquestra de violoncelos
em 3 movimentos duração - 20 minutos
Allegro- Adagio-Scher-
zando e Allegro Final

1958 - FANTASIA EM 3 MOVIMENTOS Orquestra de instrumentos Sob encomnda da " The
(em forma de choros) de sopro - duração American Wind Symphony
20 minutos. Editori Peters Co\/.

1958 - BENDITA SABEDORIA Coro misto a 6 vozes,à Palavras da Biblia
(6 Corais) capella -duração
de 20 minutos.

1958 - FANTASIA Para Saxofone Editor:Southern Music
e Orquestra Pub.
-Redução de Piano e
Saxofone
18 minutos de dura
ção.

The catalogue of new works mentioned in LETTER 80

written in Portuguese and is approximately two hours long
and therefore not *short* as the Committee desires.

Mindinha sends you, enclosed herewith, a small list of the
new works for the catalogue and asks you to forgive her not
to have done yet the rectification promised. Could you send
to Paris two copies?

Nothing more for today, with our best congratulations for
the brilliance of the Festival, the cordial embrace of your
friend,

Villa-Lobos

Villa-Lobos composing at some point in the 1950s
(courtesy of the Museu Villa-Lobos)

The last letters in the collection date from the penultimate year of Villa-Lobos' life. He had conducted in France regularly from 1948, and by the early 1950s was conducting the Orchestre National de la RTF every spring. On these occasions he would usually stay in Paris for several weeks, from 1952 onwards basing himself in the Hotel Bedford. In 1958 he was asked by Pierre Vidal,[27] President of the Club des Trois Centres,[28] to present an evening of his music. Villa-Lobos claimed that he was not a good lecturer and so, on the first Villa-Lobos evening held by the Club, 28 March 1958, in the Conservatoire Serge Rachmaninov, the music was introduced by Luiz Heitor Corrêa de Azevedo. The works heard were the *Bachianas Brasileiras* No. 9, some piano pieces, *A primeira missa no Brasil* (the finale of the Fourth Suite from *The Discovery of Brazil*) and the *Chôros* No. 10. All the orchestral pieces had been recorded under the composer's baton. After the music Villa-Lobos would reply, often expansively, to questions from the public, adding memories of his life and telling stories of other composers he had met; Bach also featured prominently in his conversation. He enjoyed the occasion so much that he asked to come again and present his Tenth Symphony, *Sumé Pater Patrium*. This he did on 29 May.

The reference to film music in LETTER 83 involves his score to the film *Green Mansions*, which was giving him some grounds for concern. He had written music that pleased him but was not suited to the minute-to-minute requirements of the company, MGM. In the event, MGM used Villa-Lobos' music not as he composed it but by having a studio composer quarry it to serve as the basis for lyrics.

---

[27] Pierre Vidal (b. 1932) is a French writer on music. For the centenary celebrations of Villa-Lobos's birth, in 1987, he helped organise concerts, radio programmes, lectures and other events in France, including the European premiere of *Genesis* (*cf.* pp. 155–60), performed by Jacques Mercier and the Orchestre National d'Île de France (the programme also contained *Erosão* and the First Piano Concerto – *cf.* pp. 139–41, 146 and 87–105).

[28] The Club des Trois Centres, founded in 1955 in conjunction with Jeunesses Musicales de France, presented little-known music in recordings, often accompanied by a talk from the artists involved. Other composers associated with the Club, besides Villa-Lobos, were Henri Dutilleux, André Jolivet, Olivier Messiaen, Maurice Ohana, Francis Poulenc and Alexandre Tcherepnin. In 1974 the Club des Trois Centres was replaced by another organisation, the Groupe des Sept, which is still active.

Concert Symphonique

consacré à la musique brésilienne
sous la direction de

HEITOR VILLA-LOBOS

LUNDI, 22 SEPTEMBRE 1958

Grand Orchestre Symphonique
de la Radiodiffusion Nationale Belge

• • •

Programme

I. Prélude (N. I. de la « Bachianas
   Brasileiras N° 4 » . . . . . H. VILLA-LOBOS.

II. « O Café » (Suite de Ballet) . . C. SANTORO.
   Abertura - Passeio - Queimada
   (Ouverture - Promenade - Queimada)

III. Symphonie N° 12 . . . . . . H. VILLA-LOBOS.
   Allegro non troppo - Adagio
   Lento - Allegro poco moderato

• • •

IV. Abertura Concertante . . . C. GUARNIERI.

V. Abertura das 3 Mascaras Perdidas   F. MIGNONE.
   (Ouverture des 3 Masques Perdus)

VI. Choros N° 6 . . . . H. VILLA-LOBOS.
   (Episode Symphonique)

The programme of the concert Villa-Lobos conducted
at the World Exhibition in Brussels

LETTER 81
VILLA-LOBOS TO PIERRE VIDAL
Original: French

Essex House
160 Central Park South
New York

6 January, 1958

Monsieur Pierre Vidal
2, Rue Fréville le Vingt
Sevres S&O[29]–France

Dear Sir,

In response to your very kind letter, I am pleased to thank the 'Club des Trois Centres' for its interest in my music and I would be delighted to be with you on the evening dedicated to my works.

Concerning the programme, I think it would be a good idea to present the Choros N. 6 and also the Choros 10 and some suite from The Discovery of Brazil, which has just received the Grand Prix du Disque in France.

I should arrive in Paris on 23 March and on this occasion you will be able to see me at the Hotel Bedford (17, Rue de l'Arcade).

Yours cordially.

H. Villa-Lobos

[29] Sèvres et Oise was later replaced by the *département* of Hauts-de-Seine (92).

LETTER 82
VILLA-LOBOS TO PIERRE VIDAL
Original: French

Hotel Bedford
17, Rue de l'Arcade
Madeleine – Paris

21 April, 1958

Monsieur Pierre Vidal
2, Rue Fréville le Vingt
Sevres S & O

Dear Mr Vidal,

In thanking you sincerely for the charming evening of the CLUB DES TROIS CENTRES which gave us so much pleasure, I would also like to thank you also for the lovely flowers you so kindly sent to my wife.

I take advantage of this opportunity to tell you that the Brazilian Embassy has borrowed[30] its tape-recorder and so you could combine the date that suits you for the session with my 10th SYMPHONY according to your wishes.

I look forward to the pleasure of seeing you again soon and send you my very affectionate thoughts.

Cordially,

H. Villa-Lobos

[30] Villa-Lobos commits a common error here, choosing the verb 'emprunter' instead of 'prêter'.

1910
Villa-Lobos takes private harmony lessons with Agnelo França and advice from composer Antônio Francisco Braga.

1911
Piano Trio No. 1, Op. 25

c. **1911–12**
Travels to Paranaguá, state of Paraná, where, for a short time, he works in a match factory, then to Belém, state of Pará, Bahia and Manaus.

1912
1 November Meets Lucília Guimarães (born 26 May 1886 in Paraíba do Sul), a pianist, teacher and, later, interpreter of his music.

Suite Infantil No. 1 for piano.

1912–13
Villa-Lobos moves to Rua Souza Neves 15 in the Tijuca area. In the afternoon he often plays cello in a small ensemble to entertain guests at the Confeitaria Colombo in Rua Gonçalves Dias, and evenings in the Assírio Restaurant in the basement of the Opera House.

Sonata Fantasia No. 1 (*Désespérance*) for violin and piano.

1913
September The Ballets Russes, on their first visit to Rio de Janeiro, perform excerpts from Borodin's *Prince Igor*, Rimsky-Korsakov's *Sheherezade*, and Debussy's *L'Après-midi d'un faune*. Music of the Russians and French Impressionists influences Villa-Lobos, who plays cello in the Theatre orchestra.

12 November Villa-Lobos marries Lucília Guimarães; they move into the home she shares with her brothers at Rua Fonseca Teles 7 in São Cristóvão area.

1914–15
Danças Características Africanas for piano solo.

1915
29 January A concert, given by Villa-Lobos, Lucília and a friend in the nearby mountain village, Nova Friburgo, includes some of

the composer's music – the first public performance of any of his music. The concert takes place at Teatro D. Eugênia.

March–June   Violoncello Concerto No. 1, Op. 50.

31 July   For the first time, some of Villa-Lobos's music – the *Suite Característica* for strings – appears in a concert programme in Rio de Janeiro, given by the Sociedade de Concêrtos Sinfônicos, conducted by Villa-Lobos's former teacher, Antônio Francisco Braga.

13 November   Villa-Lobos organises in Rio de Janeiro the first concert dedicated entirely to his own music.

1915–16
String Quartet No. 2, Op. 56

1916
Sonata No. 2, Op. 66, for cello and piano; String Quartet No. 3; Symphony No. 1, Op. 112 (*O Imprevisto*).

1917
Finishes *Miniaturas* for voice and piano. Villa-Lobos plays cello in the Odeon Movie House. He begins serious auto-didactic studies of theoretical treatises by Berlioz and Vincent d'Indy to school himself in instrumentation.

3 February   Organises the second concert with his own music.

July   Villa-Lobos' first acquaintance with the music of Stravinsky and Ravel performed by Diaghilev's visiting Ballets Russes in Rio de Janeiro.

September   Alexander Smallens conducts *Tristan and Isolde*.

17 November   Villa-Lobos organises the third concert with his own works.

Orchestral works: *Amazonas, Uírapurú, Naufrágio de Kleônikos*.

1917–18
Piano Trio No. 3

1918
Villa-Lobos, his wife and in-laws move to Rua Visconde de Parana-guá 11. He writes the fourth act of his opera *Izaht*. After meeting Arthur Rubinstein in Rio de Janeiro, he composes *A Prole do Bebê* No. 1, for piano.

15 August Villa-Lobos organises, and partly conducts, the first concert of his orchestral works.

1919
May-June He writes his Symphony No. 3 (*A Guerra*), as one of three composers commissioned by the Director of the Instituto Nacional de Música each to compose a symphony on the occasion of the commemoration of the peace treaty ending World War I.

October Villa-Lobos sketches his Symphony No. 4 (*A Vitória*) and plans his Symphony No. 5 (*A Paz*).

Villa-Lobos leaves the home of his in-laws and, together with his wife, moves to Rua Didimo 10 in the Tijuca area, the couple's home until May 1936. Beginning of public recognition: conductors and soloists occasionally include his music in their concert programmes.

1919–20
Carnaval das Crianças Brasileiras.

1920 and 1922
Felix Weingartner conducts music by Wagner in Rio de Janeiro and includes *Naufrágio de Kleônikos* and *Dança Frenética* in his concerts.

1920 and 1923
Richard Strauss conducts his compositions in Rio de Janeiro.

1921
Boris Godunov and other Russian music performed in Rio de Janeiro. Vera Janacópulos sings three songs from *Miniaturas* in Paris, the first time Villa-Lobos's music is heard there.

Quatuor, Epigramas Irônicos e Sentimentais, A Prole do Bebê No. 2.

1922
During a 'Week of Modern Art' in São Paulo Brazilian contempor-ary and avant-garde writers, poets, painters and composers organise

lectures, recitals and exhibitions – including three recitals (13, 15 and 17 February) of Villa-Lobos' music – to promote Brazilian art and music.

Villa-Lobos obtains a grant from the Brazilian government for a one-year sojourn in Paris.

1923
Poème de l'enfant et de sa mère, Nonetto.

30 June   Villa-Lobos embarks for Europe on the S.S. Croix.

1924
15 February   Villa-Lobos conducts a concert in Paris of music of Latin American composers, although he performs none of his own.

9 and 16 March   Villa-Lobos conducts Brazilian music, this time including his own, with the Orquestra Sinfônica Portuguêsa at the Teatro São Luiz in Lisbon.

28 March   Conducts Brazilian music in the Musée Galliéra in Paris.

3 April   Gives a concert in Brussels.

4 April and 11 April   During the Exposition d'Art Américain Latin in the Musée Galliéra Villa-Lobos' music is played.

9 April   The Sixth Jean Wiéner Concert includes Villa-Lobos' Trio for oboe, clarinet and bassoon (1921).

30 May   Villa-Lobos conducts his works and premieres his *Nonetto* in the Salle des Agriculteurs – his most important Paris concert to date.

In the summer Villa-Lobos returns to Rio de Janeiro. The great breakthrough: he creates his own musical style.

Chôros Nos. 2 and 7.

8 October   Villa-Lobos signs his first contract with the Paris publishing house Éditions Max Eschig. Previous works were published mainly by Arthur Napoleão in Rio de Janeiro.

1925
January and February Villa-Lobos conducts Brazilian and French music in São Paulo and on 18 and 20 February a concert with his own works which meets with success.

Chóros No. 3.

1 and 17 June Attends two chamber music concerts of his works in Buenos Aires. Upon his return to Rio de Janeiro he writes *Chōros* Nos. 5 and 8.

30 November and 5 December Presents his new compositions in São Paulo.

1926
Arranges concert of his music in Rio de Janeiro. He persistently organises concerts to present his latest works since others appear uninterested in including his music in their programmes.

31 October, 15 and 19 November Gives three more concerts.

December Embarks for Paris with Lucília, supported by Arnaldo and Carlos Guinle, two Brazilian industrialists, to spend three-and-a-half years in France.

Chansons Typiques Brésiliennes, Três Poemas Indígenas, Serestas, Cirandas, Chôros Nos. 4 and 10.

1927
January Villa-Lobos settles at 11 place St. Michel. Begins to arrange and edit the Guinle brothers' collection of folk- and children's songs. Publication, financed by the Guinles, is foreseen, but no publisher is found. The collection is never returned to its owners, the Guinles; its whereabouts have since remained unknown.

Villa-Lobos signs a further contract with Éditions Max Eschig. Meets Stokowski, Albert Wolff, Edgard Varèse and Florent Schmitt, then music critic of *Le Temps*; Schmitt becomes a staunch admirer of Villa-Lobos' music.

24 October and 5 December Villa-Lobos presents his latest compositions with the Orchestre Colonne at the Maison Gaveau.

1928
23 and 24 November Stokowski and the Philadelphia Orchestra perform Villa-Lobos' *Danças Características Africanas* in Philadelphia and, on 27 November, at Carnegie Hall in New York. Presumably the first time that North American audiences hear a work by Villa-Lobos.

Quintetto em forma de Chôros, Twelve Études and *Suite Populaire* for guitar.

1929
21 January Signs a further contract with Éditions Max Eschig.

2 and 3 February Albert Wolff and the Concerts Lamoureux perform *Chôros* No. 8. The composer writes *Deux Chôros (Bis), Suite Suggestive.*

During the summer Villa-Lobos takes a vacation in Brazil and conducts a series of concerts in Rio de Janeiro and São Paulo.

Mômoprecóce.

In early October Villa-Lobos embarks for Barcelona to conduct, on 18 October, Brazilian music including his own; then he travels to Paris.

1930
25 January and 21 March Further contracts with Éditions Max Eschig.

23 February Villa-Lobos's *Mômoprecóce* is premiered in Salle Pleyel, Paris, with the Brazilian soloist Magda Tagliaferro.

1 April Villa-Lobos attends a chamber-music concert at Liège.

3 April and 7 May In the Salle Gaveau Villa-Lobos presents his newest compositions. At the end of May, he and Lucília leave Paris for Brazil. He is not to return to France until after World War II.
During the second half of the year Villa-Lobos gives a series of concerts in São Paulo including his own works, interrupted only by Brazil's October Revolution, with its forebodings of nationalist tendencies. The composer begins his *Bachianas Brasileiras* series.

1931
Villa-Lobos, together with a group of other musicians, undertakes a musical pilgrimage into the hinterland of São Paulo organised in conjunction with the respective municipalities, offering music in places otherwise deprived of cultural events.

24 May At the Campo São Bento in São Paulo Villa-Lobos conducts his first mass chorus with unexpected success. This marks the beginning of the composer's interest in choral singing and choral arrangements of folk- and children's songs.

With his group of musicians Villa-Lobos visits the São Paulo hinterland twice. Upon his return to the city of São Paulo, he conducts two more concerts on 6 and 21 October which include his newest choral arrangements. At the end of the year he finally settles in Rio de Janeiro.

String Quartet No. 5.

1932
18 April SEMA (Superintendência de Educação Musical Artística do Departamento de Educação da Prefeitura do [então] Distrito Federal) is established by decree, to make choral singing in municipal schools mandatory. Villa-Lobos is nominated head of SEMA, a post specifically created for him. For the first time in his life, Villa-Lobos, now aged 45, has a secure monthly income. He forms his music teachers' chorus, called Orfeão de Professores.

Caixinha de Boas Festas.

1933
The composer creates the Villa-Lobos Orchestra, dismantled the following year for lack of funds, and conducts unorthodox programmes.

1934
18 and 20 June On the occasion of the South American Theosophical Congress Villa-Lobos conducts two concerts.

1935
In connection with his SEMA activities, Villa-Lobos organises a number of concerts between August and December.

1936

25 April   Villa-Lobos attends the First International Congress for Musical Education in Prague and returns via Berlin and Barcelona to Rio de Janeiro.

28 May   Villa-Lobos decides to separate from his wife Lucília and leaves their home.

Ciclo Brasileiro.

1937
Descobrimento do Brasil, Missa São Sebastião.

1938
Villa-Lobos composes the first movement of his *Bachianas Brasileiras* No. 5; it is to become his most celebrated piece of music. The second movement is composed seven years later.

1939
4–9 May   At the World Fair in New York Villa-Lobos' music is heard during a festival of Brazilian music.

As Três Marias.

1940
16–20 October   At a further Festival of Brazilian music, held at the Museum of Modern Art in New York, Villa-Lobos' music is performed. The composer gives concerts at Montevideo, Uruguay and Buenos Aires.

1942
July   First performances of *Chôros* Nos. 6, 9 and 11 in Rio de Janeiro.

In Rio de Janeiro Villa-Lobos launches the Conservatório Nacional de Canto Orfeônico which is established by decree on 26 November.

Bachianas Brasileiras No. 7.

1944
21 November   Receives the honorary doctorate in law from Occidental College.

26 November   Villa-Lobos' American debut in Los Angeles with the Werner Janssen Symphony Orchestra has little success.

Bachianas Brasileiras No. 8, String Quartet No. 8.

1945
28 January The League of Composers offers a chamber music concert of Villa-Lobos' music at New York's Museum of Modern Art.

8 and 9 February Villa-Lobos's first New York appearance with the Philharmonic Orchestra is followed by appearances in Boston and Chicago.

14 July Villa-Lobos launches the Brazilian Academy of Music in Rio de Janeiro.

Fantasia for cello and orchestra, *Bachianas Brasileiras* No. 9, Piano Concerto No. 1, Symphony No. 7, *Madona*.

1946
13 March Villa-Lobos' mother, Noêmia, dies.

1947
After a visit to Rome, Villa-Lobos travels to New York to receive from Edwin Lester, President of the Los Angeles Civic Light Opera Association, a commission to write the operetta *Magdalena*. From now until the end of his life, the composer lives part of every year in the United States, Europe and Brazil, and guest-conducts in other Latin American countries.

1948
9 July Villa-Lobos enters the Memorial Hospital in New York for an operation for cancer of the bladder.

1950
String Quartet No. 12

1951
Guitar Concerto.

1952
Villa-Lobos chooses the Hotel Bedford in Paris for his European headquarters.

17–19 June Villa-Lobos conducts the Israel Philharmonic Orchestra.

Symphony No. 10, Piano Concerto No. 4.

1953
Odisséia de uma Raça, Fantasia Concertante, Harp Concerto, *Alvorada na Floresta Tropical,* String Quartet No. 14, Cello Concerto No. 2.

1954
Piano Concerto No. 5, String Quartet No. 15.

1955
Symphony No. 11, Harmonica Concerto.

1955–56
Basil Langton commissions Villa-Lobos to compose music for a ballet, based on Eugene O'Neill's *The Emperor Jones,* and John Blankenship commissions the composer to set Federico García Lorca's play *Yerma* to music.

1957
Symphony No. 12, *Quinteto Instrumental,* String Quartet No. 17.

On the occasion of his seventieth birthday, Villa-Lobos is made an honorary citizen of São Paulo where, in September, a festival with his music during a 'Villa-Lobos week' takes place. The Brazilian government declares 1957 'Villa-Lobos Year'.

1958
MGM commissions Villa-Lobos to write the music for the film *Green Mansions,* based on the novel by W. H. Hudson.

A Menina das Nuvens, Bendita Sabedoria, Magnificat Aleluia.

3 December The University of New York confers an honorary doctorate on Villa-Lobos.

1959
12 July In Bear Mountains, Villa-Lobos conducts the last concert of his life.

14 July In Rio de Janeiro Villa-Lobos receives the Carlos Gomes Medal.

11 August Villa-Lobos, in hospital in Rio de Janeiro for uraemia and kidney congestion, makes his will.

7 September   Villa-Lobos, attends the last concert of his life at the Municipal Theatre to hear his *Magnificat Aleluia*.

17 November   Villa-Lobos dies, aged 72, at his home in the Rua Araújo, Pôrto Alegre 56, Apt. 54, in Rio de Janeiro.

1960
From February to April, the New York Public Library holds an exhibit in Villa-Lobos' memory with photos, recordings, scores, books.

1961
20 January   The Museu Villa-Lobos in Rio de Janeiro – established by decree in June 1960 – opens its doors under the direction of Arminda Villa-Lobos, the composer's companion during the last 23 years of his life. Ever since its opening the Museum has arranged festivals and competitions and publishes books and recordings.

1966
25 May   Villa-Lobos' wife, Lucília, dies.

1971
5 March   On the occasion of the 84th anniversary of Villa-Lobos' birth, a memorial plate is affixed to the Hotel Bedford in Paris.

12 August   Premiere of *Yerma* at Santa Fe Opera, Santa Fe, New Mexico.

1985
5 August   Arminda d'Almeida Villa-Lobos (born 26 July 1912) dies, aged 73, in Rio de Janeiro.

Appendix Two

RALPH GUSTAFSON
ON VILLA-LOBOS

This Appendix contains the bulk of two letters from the Canadian poet Ralph Gustafson written in response to my enquiries in the preparation of this book. The first was dated 28 January 1984, the second 23 February 1984. They reveal aspects of Villa-Lobos' character which his own correspondence almost entirely disguises.

Your inquiry about Villa-Lobos came this morning. A strange conjunction. I had just finished typing a new poem into my MS which McClelland & Stewart of Toronto is bringing out in the near future under the title 'New Poems'. The poem is titled 'The Broken Pianola' – a metaphor I rescued from the back of my mind to symbolize our world's present age. The image goes back to September 1948 when Villa-Lobos' musical *Magdalena* was presented at the Ziegfeld Theatre in New York City. Villa-Lobos was conducting and I shall not forget the astoundingly effective and original number when the ballet danced to the Villa-Lobos music on the mechanical player piano – and every time the machine broke down the complete scene – dancers and pit-orchestra – stopped dead too!

What a loss that Villa-Lobos' musical was never revived – a musical far and away superior to anything on Broadway at the time – and, almost, since. Irra Petina, John Raitt and Dorothy Sarnoff were in the original cast. It was my guess that the run was short because of the 'religious' basis of the musical.[1]

All this as prologue to saying that I remember your study of Villa-Lobos' music in *The Music Review*, 'Some Aspects of Villa-

---

[1] In the event, *Magdalena* was revived for a concert performance in New Haven, Connecticut, and in the Alice Tully Hall, Lincoln Center, New York, to celebrate the Villa-Lobos centenary in 1987; that production, conducted by Evans Haile, was recorded and released on compact disc on CBS MK 44945.

Appendix Three
BIBLIOGRAPHY

This bibliography lists only the more important recent writings on Villa-Lobos, largely those in English which are relevant to matters discussed in this book.

ANON., *Villa-Lobos – Sua Obra*, Museu Villa-Lobos, Rio de Janeiro, 1965, 2nd edn., 1972; 3rd edn., 1989.

——, *Villa-Lobos, Visto da Platéia e na Intimidade, 1912/1935*, published privately, Rio de Janeiro, 1972.

APPLEBY, DAVID P., *Heitor Villa-Lobos: A Bio-Bibliography*, Greenwood Press, Westport and London, 1988.

AZEVEDO, LUIZ HEITOR CORRÊA DE, 'Villa-Lobos', in *The New Grove Dictionary of Music and Musicians*, Macmillan, London, 1980, Vol. 19, pp. 763–67.

GUSTAFSON, RALPH, 'Villa-Lobos and the Man-eating Flower: A Memoir', *The Musical Quarterly*, Spring 1991, Vol. 75, No. 1, pp. 1–11.

HORTA, LUÍS PAULO, *Heitor Villa-Lobos*, Edições Alumbramento: Livroarte Editora, Rio de Janeiro; 1986.

MARIZ, VASCO, *Heitor Villa-Lobos, compositor brasileiro*, Zahar, Rio de Janeiro, 1983.

NOGUEIRA FRANÇA, EURICO, *Villa-Lobos, Síntese Crítica e Biográfica*, Museu Villa-Lobos, Rio de Janeiro, 3rd edn., 1978.

PEPPERCORN, LISA M., *Heitor Villa-Lobos: Ein Komponist aus Brasilien*, Atlantis, Zurich, 1972.

——, 'Villa-Lobos's Brazilian Excursions', *The Musical Times*, cxiii, No. 1549, March 1972, pp. 263–65.

——, 'The Fifteen-Year Periods in Villa-Lobos's Life', *Ibero-Amerikanisches Archiv*, Vol. 5, No. 2, 1979, pp. 179–97.

——, 'Villa-Lobos's Last Years', *The Music Review*, Vol. 40, No. 4, November 1979, pp. 285–99.

——, 'Correspondence between H. Villa-Lobos and his Wife Lucília', *Music and Letters*, Vol. 61, Nos. 3/4, July/October 1980, pp. 284–92.

——, 'A Villa-Lobos Autograph Letter at the Bibliothèque Nationale'. *The Latin American Music Review*, Vol. 1, No. 2, October 1980, pp. 253–64.

——, 'A Letter from Villa-Lobos to Arnaldo Guinle', *Studi Musicali*, Vol. X. No. 1, 1981, pp. 171–79.

——, 'The Paris Bibliothèque Nationale's Autograph Letter of Villa-Lobos to his Sponsor', *The Journal of Musicological Research*, Nos. 3/4, 1981, pp. 423–33.

——, 'Villa-Lobos's Stage Works', *Revue Belge de Musicologie*, Vol. XXXVI–XXXVIII, 1982–84, pp. 175–84.

——, 'Menschen, Masken, Mythen: Heitor Villa-Lobos und die brasilianische Musik', *Neue Zeitschrift für Musik*, September 1984, pp. 8–11.

——, 'Villa-Lobos's Commissioned Compositions', *Tempo*, No. 151, December 1984, pp. 28–31.

——, 'Villa-Lobos in Paris', *The Latin American Music Review*, Vol. 6, No. 2, October 1985, pp. 235–48.

——, 'The Villa-Lobos Family', *The Music Review*, Vol. 49, No. 2, 1988, pp. 134–37.

——, 'Villa-Lobos in Israel', *Tempo*, No. 169, June 1989, pp. 42–45.

——, *Villa-Lobos* (The Illustrated Lives of the Great Composers), Omnibus Press, London, 1989.

——, *Villa-Lobos – The Music: An Analysis of his Style*, Kahn & Averill, London, 1991.

——, 'Villa-Lobos "Ben Trovato"', *Tempo*, No. 177, June 1991, pp. 32–39.

——, *Villa-Lobos: Collected Studies*, Scolar Press, Aldershot, 1992.

ROUND, MICHAEL, '*Bachianas Brasileiras* in Performance', *Tempo*, No. 169, June 1989, pp. 34–41.

RUBINSKY, SONIA, *Villa-Lobos's Rudepoêma: An Analysis*, PhD. dissertation, The Juilliard School, New York, 1986.

SCHIC, ANNA STELLA, *Villa-Lobos, Souvenirs de l'Indien Blanc*, Actes Sud, Arles, 1987.

WRIGHT, SIMON, *Villa-Lobos and his Position in Brazilian Music after 1930*, PhD. dissertation, University College, Cardiff, 1986.

——, *Villa-Lobos*, Oxford Studies of Composers, Clarendon Press, Oxford, 1992.

Index
of Works

201

General
Index

208 General Index

School of African and Oriental
Studies, 106n
Schott' & Sons, B.

, 26
Schuman, William, 139n, 160n
Schwerké, Irving, 10, 14, 23, 24,
27, 28, 36, 115, 116, 120, 121,
122, 123, 124, 125, 126
Views and Interviews, 122, 123
Sebastian, John, 166n
Second Empire, 27n
Segáll, Bernardo, 14, 138, 139, 180
Seattle, 156n
Seiber, Mátyás, 106n
Sèvres et Oise, 177n
Slonimsky, Nicolas, 14, 69, 70, 71,
72
Music of Latin America, 71
Perfect Pitch, 70n
Smallens, Alexander, 184
Smith, Carleton Sprague, 167
Sociedade de Concêrtos Sinfônicos,
184
Sociedade Sinfônica de São Paulo,
44n
South America, 100, 165n
South American Theosophical
Congress, 189
Southern California, University of,
138
Spivacke, Harold, 14, 78, 80, 81
Stokowski, Leopold, 24, 133, 187,
188
Strauss, Richard, 185
Stravinsky, Igor, 184
Studi Musicali, 15
Sugar Loaf Moutain, 129
Superintendência de Educação
Musical e Artística, 50, 64, 189
Switzerland, 164n

Tachau, Louise, 149
Tagliaferro, Magda, 30, 188
Tanglewood, 82

Tansman, Alexandre, 98n, 106n
Tcherepnin, Alexandre, 175n
Tennessee, University of, 165n
Teixeira, Anísio Spinola, 52
Temps, Le, 43, 187
Terán, Tomás, 34
Tertis, Lionel, 97n
Thompson, Virgil, 139n
Tilden Foundation, 14
Toronto, 98, 102, 194

UNESCO, 115, 126, 127
United States, 24, 65, 75, 76, 82,
85, 87, 95, 116, 120, 121, 123,
126, 133, 134, 136, 165n, 167,
170, 180, 191
Information Agency, 169, 170
State Department, 165n, 169
Urban, Mrs, 95

Van Vactor, David, 165
Varèse, Edgard, 187,
Vargas, Getúlio Dornelles, 38, 43, 64
Venezuela, 126
Vidal, Pierre, 9, 15, 175, 177, 178,
179
Vienna, 19, 126, 165n
Vieuxtemps, Henri, 30n
Villa-Lobos, Arminda (Mindinha)
d'Almeida, 14, 15, 30n, 63, 83,
88, 91, 93, 95, 96, 97, 99, 104n,
105n, 123, 129, 137, 159, 173,
193, 195, 196, 197n
Villa-Lobos, Francisco da Silveira,
181
Villa-Lobos, Heitor, *passim*
Villa-Lobos, Lucília Guimarães, 9,
10, 12, 15, 19, 26, 30, 43, 44,
46, 47, 50, 51, 53, 54, 56–63,
183, 185, 187, 188, 190, 193
Villa-Lobos, Maria Carolina
Serzedelo, 181